Brilliant Business Strategic Management

Niall McCreanor , M.B.S

For Jacinta, Oisín, Erin and Faolán

My World!

Contents

3

i. Introduction to Business Management Strategy

Business management strategy is a critical component of any successful organisation. As noted by Mintzberg et al. (2005), strategy involves "a pattern in a stream of decisions" that defines the organisation's goals and objectives and guides its actions and operations over time. In other words, strategy is about making choices that create a sustainable competitive advantage for the organisation (Porter, 1996).

This chapter gives an overview of business management strategy, including why it's important and how it applies to organisations of all sizes and types. We start by talking about what strategy is and its most important parts, such as vision, mission, goals, and objectives. Then, we look at the different kinds of strategies that companies can use, such as differentiation, cost leadership, and focus (Porter, 1980).

Next, we explore the role of strategic planning in organisations and how it can help to align goals and objectives with actions and operations. We also talk about how important implementation and evaluation are in strategic planning, as well as how important it is to keep getting better and change with the times (Ansoff, 1987).

In the last part of the chapter, we talk about how important business management strategy is in today's complex and changing business world. We argue (Mintzberg et al., 2005) that organisations that don't make and use good strategies are less likely to survive and do well in the long run.

Why Business Management Strategy Matters

Business management strategy is important for the success of any company, no matter how big or what industry it is in. Porter (1996) said that strategy is about making decisions that give the organisation a competitive advantage that can last. In other words, strategy helps organisations to focus their resources and efforts on the activities that are most likely to lead to success.

One of the key reasons why business management strategy matters is that it provides a framework for decision-making. By defining the organisation's goals and objectives, strategy helps managers to prioritise their actions and allocate resources effectively (Mintzberg et al., 2005). Without a clear strategy, organisations may struggle to make decisions that are aligned with their overall vision and mission.

Another reason why business management strategy matters is that it helps organisations to adapt to changing circumstances. In today's dynamic business environment, organisations must be able to respond quickly to new opportunities and threats (Ansoff, 1987). A well-defined strategy can help organisations to anticipate and respond to changes in the market, industry, or competitive landscape.

Finally, business management strategy matters because it helps to create a sense of direction and purpose for the organisation. By defining the organisation's vision and mission, strategy provides a clear sense of what the organisation stands for and what it is trying to achieve (Kaplan & Norton, 2008). This can be a powerful motivator for employees and stakeholders, helping to create a shared sense of purpose and commitment.

Business management strategy matters because it provides a framework for decision-making, helps organisations to adapt to changing circumstances, and creates a sense of direction and purpose for the organisation. Without a clear strategy, organisations may struggle to achieve their goals and objectives, and may be at risk of falling behind their competitors.

Overview of Business Management Strategy

(Mintzberg et al., 2005) say that a business management strategy is a set of decisions and actions that a company takes to reach its goals and objectives. It means figuring out what the organisation's vision and mission are, setting goals and objectives, and making sure that resources and actions are aligned to reach those goals. Effective business management strategy can help organisations to create a sustainable competitive advantage and achieve long-term success (Porter, 1996).

One of the key components of business management strategy is vision. The vision statement describes the organisation's desired future state and helps to inspire and motivate employees and stakeholders (Kaplan & Norton, 2008). A well-crafted vision statement can help to create a sense of purpose and direction for the organisation.

Another important component of business management strategy is mission. The mission statement describes the organisation's purpose and core values, and provides a framework for decision-making and action (Kaplan & Norton, 2008). A clear mission statement can help to ensure that all stakeholders are aligned around a common set of goals and objectives.

Setting goals and objectives is also part of a business management strategy, along with having a vision and mission. Ansoff (1987) says that goals are broad statements of what the organisation wants to do, while objectives are specific, measurable, and time-bound goals. Effective goals and objectives can help to focus the organisation's efforts and resources on the most important activities.

Lastly, a business management strategy involves making sure that the organisation's actions and resources are in line with its goals and objectives. (Mintzberg et al., 2005) This could mean coming up with specific strategies and tactics for each goal and allocating resources in a way that helps these strategies work. Effective alignment can help make sure that the organisation makes the most of its resources and meets its goals and objectives in the most efficient and effective way possible.

Business management strategy is a set of decisions and actions that organisations take to achieve their goals and objectives. It involves defining the organisation's vision and mission, setting goals and objectives, and aligning resources and actions to achieve them. Effective business management strategy can help organisations to create a sustainable competitive advantage and achieve long-term success.

Importance of Business Management Strategy in Today's Business Environment

In today's complex and changing business world, it is more important than ever to come up with a good business management strategy. Companies face a range of challenges, including rapid technological change, evolving customer preferences, and intense competition, and a well-developed business management strategy can help companies to navigate these challenges and achieve sustained success.

One of the most important things about business management strategy is that it helps companies stay competitive in a market that is always changing. By developing strategies that are aligned with market trends and customer needs, companies can position themselves for success and outperform competitors (Porter, 1996). In addition, an effective business management strategy can help companies to mitigate risks and capitalise on opportunities, enabling them to adapt to changing market conditions and stay ahead of the curve.

A good business management strategy also gives companies a way to make decisions and helps them focus their resources on strategic priorities. By developing a clear mission statement, defining business goals and objectives, and prioritising strategic initiatives, companies can ensure that their resources are directed towards activities that contribute to long-term success (Kaplan & Norton, 2001).

Finally, an effective business management strategy can also help to enhance organisational alignment and improve communication and collaboration within the organisation. By developing a shared understanding of strategic priorities and aligning organisational activities with these priorities, companies can promote a sense of unity and purpose within the organisation, enhancing employee motivation and engagement (Kotter & Heskett, 1992).

In today's complex and changing business world, companies that want to be successful over the long term need to develop an effective business management strategy. By staying competitive, mitigating risks, and capitalising on opportunities, companies can adapt to changing market conditions and outperform competitors, while promoting organisational alignment and enhancing employee motivation and engagement.

ii. Analysing Your Business Environment

Before making a plan for running a business, it's important to take a close look at the business environment. The business environment includes a range of factors that can impact the organisation's performance and success, including the industry and market, competitors, and opportunities and threats (Ansoff, 1987).

This chapter provides an overview of the key elements of analysing your business environment. We begin by discussing the importance of understanding your industry and market. This involves identifying the key trends and drivers in the industry, as well as understanding the needs and preferences of your customers (Porter, 1980).

Next, we examine the role of competitors in the business environment. Analysing your competitors involves identifying their strengths and weaknesses, as well as understanding their strategies and tactics (Porter, 1980). This information can help organisations to develop effective competitive strategies and differentiate themselves from their competitors.

Finally, we discuss the importance of analysing opportunities and threats in the business environment. Opportunities may arise from changes in the market or industry, while threats may arise from competitive pressures or other external factors (Ansoff, 1987). By analysing these factors, organisations can identify potential areas for growth and development, as well as potential risks and challenges.

Analysing your business environment is a key part of making a good plan for managing your business. By knowing their industry, market, competitors, opportunities, and threats, organisations can come up with strategies that fit their business environment and help them be successful in the long run.

Understanding Your Industry and Market

Understanding your industry and market is one of the most important parts of analysing your business environment. The industry and market are critical factors that can impact the organisation's performance and success (Porter, 1980). Understanding the industry

20

and market involves identifying the key trends and drivers in the industry, as well as understanding the needs and preferences of your customers.

It is important to do a thorough analysis of the outside world in order to understand your industry and market. This may involve using tools such as SWOT analysis, PESTLE analysis, and Porter's Five Forces analysis (Porter, 1980). These tools can help organisations to identify the key factors that are shaping the industry and market, as well as the opportunities and threats that exist.

The competitive landscape is an important thing to think about when analysing your industry and market. This means figuring out who the main competitors are and what their strengths and weaknesses are (Porter, 1980). By understanding the competitive landscape, businesses can come up with good strategies to beat their competitors and set themselves apart.

Another important factor to consider is the needs and preferences of your customers. This may involve conducting market research to understand the demographics, behaviours, and attitudes of your target customers (Kotler & Keller, 2016). By understanding the needs and preferences of your customers, organisations can develop

21

products and services that meet their needs and preferences and that are well-aligned with the market.

Understanding your industry and market is a critical component of analysing your business environment. By identifying the key trends and drivers in the industry, as well as understanding the needs and preferences of your customers, organisations can develop effective strategies that are well-aligned with the external environment and that enable them to achieve long-term success.

Identifying and Analysing Competitors

Competitors are an important part of the business environment that can affect how well and how well an organisation does. Understanding your competitors involves identifying their strengths and weaknesses, as well as understanding their strategies and tactics (Porter, 1980). By analysing your competitors, you can develop effective competitive strategies and differentiate yourself from your competitors.

One way to identify your competitors is to conduct a competitor analysis. A competitor analysis involves gathering information about your competitors, including their products and services, market share, and pricing strategies (Porter, 1980). This information can be gathered through a variety of sources, including market research, public filings, and industry reports.

Once you know who your competitors are, you need to figure out what their strengths and weaknesses are. This could mean looking at how well they do financially, how they market and sell their products, and how their supply chain and operations work (Porter, 1980). By knowing the strengths and weaknesses of your competitors, you can come up with plans that take advantage of their weaknesses and make the most of your own strengths.

Another important factor to consider when analysing your competitors is their strategies and tactics. This may involve assessing their marketing and advertising campaigns, their pricing strategies, and their product development strategies (Porter, 1980). By understanding your competitors' strategies and tactics, you can develop strategies that differentiate yourself from your competitors and that meet the needs and preferences of your customers.

Identifying and analysing competitors is a critical component of analysing your business environment. By understanding your competitors' strengths and weaknesses, as well as their strategies and tactics, you can develop effective competitive strategies and differentiate yourself from your competitors.

Assessing Opportunities and Threats

Assessing opportunities and threats is a critical component of analysing your business environment. Opportunities may arise from changes in the market or industry, while threats may arise from competitive pressures or other external factors (Ansoff, 1987). By analysing these factors, organisations can identify potential areas for growth and development, as well as potential risks and challenges.

One way to assess opportunities and threats is to conduct a SWOT analysis, which stands for strengths, weaknesses, opportunities, and threats. Kotler and Keller (2016) say that this analysis is about finding the internal and external factors that affect the performance and success of the organisation. By conducting a SWOT analysis, organisations can identify potential areas for improvement, as well as potential areas of risk and vulnerability.

In the "strengths" section, for example, a company might list its highly skilled and experienced employees or its strong brand reputation. In the "weaknesses" section, an organisation might list things that need to be fixed, like old technology or a lack of resources. In the "opportunities" section, an organisation might list new trends or untapped markets. In the "threats" section, it might list possible risks like more competition or new rules.

A PESTLE analysis is another way to figure out what the opportunities and risks are. PESTLE stands for political, economic, social, technological, legal, and environmental factors. This analysis involves analysing the external environment in which the organisation operates (Kotler & Keller, 2016). By conducting a PESTLE analysis, organisations can identify potential opportunities and threats arising from changes in the external environment.

For example, in the "political" category, an organisation may consider changes in government policies or regulations that could impact its operations. In the "economic" category, it may consider changes in interest rates or currency exchange rates. In the "social" category, it may consider changes in consumer attitudes or demographics. In the "technological" category, it may consider advancements in automation or artificial intelligence. In the "legal" category, it may consider changes in laws or regulations that could impact its operations. In the "environmental" category, it may consider changes in climate or natural resources that could impact its operations.

Organisations can look at opportunities and threats with more than just SWOT and PESTLE analyses. For example, Porter's Five Forces model (Porter, 1980) is a way to look at how competitive forces affect an organisation. Organisations can come up with long-term plans for success if they understand the competitive forces in their industry.

For example, in Porter's Five Forces model, organisations look at the bargaining power of suppliers, the bargaining power of buyers, the threat of new entrants, the threat of substitutes, and the intensity of competitive rivalry. By identifying the strengths and weaknesses of these forces, organisations can develop strategies that enable them to gain a competitive advantage.

Assessing opportunities and threats is a critical component of analysing your business environment. By conducting SWOT and PESTLE analyses, as well as using other tools and frameworks such as Porter's Five Forces model, organisations can identify potential areas for growth and development, as well as potential risks and challenges. This information can then be used to develop effective business management strategies that enable the organisation to achieve long-term success.

Assessing opportunities and threats is a key part of analysing the business environment and coming up with a good strategy for managing a business. By figuring out where there might be room for growth and development, as well as where there might be risks and challenges, organisations can make well-informed decisions and come up with strategies that work well with the outside world. SWOT and PESTLE analyses are valuable tools that can help organisations to identify internal and external factors that impact their performance and success, while Porter's Five Forces model can help organisations to identify competitive forces in the industry. Overall, assessing opportunities and threats is essential for organisations seeking to achieve long-term success in a dynamic and competitive business environment.

iii.   Defining Your Business Strategy

After you have done a thorough analysis of your business environment, the next step is to define your business strategy. Business strategy is the set of decisions and actions that determine the long-term direction and success of the organisation (Hitt, Ireland, & Hoskisson, 2017). Developing an effective business strategy requires a clear understanding of the organisation's goals, resources, and capabilities, as well as the external environment in which it operates.

This chapter provides an overview of the key elements of defining your business strategy. We begin by discussing the importance of establishing clear goals and objectives. This involves setting specific, measurable, achievable, relevant, and time-bound (SMART) goals that align with the organisation's mission and vision (Hitt, Ireland, & Hoskisson, 2017).

Next, we examine the role of resources and capabilities in defining your business strategy. Resources include the financial, human, and physical assets of the organisation, while capabilities refer to the organisation's skills, knowledge, and expertise (Hitt, Ireland, & Hoskisson, 2017). By understanding its resources and capabilities, an organisation can develop strategies that leverage its strengths and mitigate its weaknesses.

Finally, we discuss the importance of aligning your business strategy with the external environment. This involves developing strategies that are responsive to changes in the industry and market, as well as the needs and preferences of your customers (Porter, 1980). By aligning your business strategy with the external environment, organisations can develop strategies that are well-suited to their specific context and that enable them to achieve long-term success.

Defining your business strategy is an important part of making a good plan for running a business. Organisations can create strategies that are well-aligned with their mission and vision and help them achieve long-term success by setting clear goals and objectives, knowing their resources and abilities, and making sure their strategy fits with the outside world.

Developing a Mission Statement

A mission statement is a concise statement that summarises the purpose and values of the organisation. It serves as a guide for decision-making and provides a sense of direction and identity for the organisation (Collins & Porras, 1996). Developing a mission statement is an important step in defining your business strategy, as it helps to clarify the organisation's purpose and priorities.

To make a mission statement, it's important to get people from different parts of the organisation involved. Collins and Porras (1996) say that this could include employees, customers, and other key stakeholders who have a stake in the success of the organisation. By involving stakeholders, organisations can make sure that the mission statement reflects the organisation's overall values and priorities.

Using a framework like the "Mission, Vision, and Values" framework is one way to come up with a mission statement. This means making a clear mission statement that explains the organisation's goals and priorities, a vision statement that describes the organisation's ideal future, and a set of core values that guide the organisation's decisions (Collins & Porras, 1996).

Mission, Vision, and Values Framework

The Mission, Vision, and Values framework is a widely used approach to developing a clear and concise statement of an organisation's purpose, priorities, and values (Collins & Porras, 1996). This framework involves developing a mission statement that summarises the organisation's purpose and priorities, a vision statement that describes the desired future state of the organisation, and a set of core values that guide the organisation's decision-making.

Mission Statement

The mission statement is a concise statement that summarises the organisation's purpose and priorities. It should be clear, specific, and well-defined, and should reflect the unique identity and values of the organisation (Collins & Porras, 1996). The mission statement should also be relevant to the organisation's stakeholders, including customers, employees, and investors.

For example, the mission statement of Coca-Cola Company is "To refresh the world in mind, body, and spirit, to inspire moments of optimism and happiness, and to create value and make a difference" (Coca-Cola Company, 2022). This mission statement reflects the organisation's focus on providing refreshing beverages that bring joy and happiness to its customers.

Vision Statement

The vision statement describes the desired future state of the organisation. It should be aspirational, inspiring, and aligned with the organisation's mission and values (Collins & Porras, 1996). The vision statement should also be achievable and realistic, and should provide a clear direction for the organisation's long-term goals and priorities.

For example, the vision statement of Tesla is "To accelerate the world's transition to sustainable energy" (Tesla, 2022). This vision statement shows that the organisation's main goal is to come up with sustainable energy solutions that can reduce the amount of carbon dioxide that transportation uses.

Values Statement

The values statement outlines the core values and beliefs that guide the organisation's decision-making. It should be clear, specific, and well-defined, and should reflect the unique identity and culture of the organisation (Collins & Porras, 1996). The values statement should also be relevant to the organisation's stakeholders, including customers, employees, and investors.

For example, the values statement of Google is "Do the right thing. Focus on the user. And every once in a while, it doesn't hurt to think big" (Google, 2022). This values statement reflects the organisation's focus on ethical and user-centred decision-making, as well as its culture of innovation and creativity.

Another way is to focus on making a mission statement that is short, easy to remember, and clear. This may involve using language that is simple and clear, and that reflects the organisation's unique identity and values (Kotler & Keller, 2016). A well-crafted mission statement can serve as a rallying cry for the organisation and can help to align employees and stakeholders around a common purpose.

Developing a mission statement is a critical step in defining your business strategy. By involving stakeholders in the process and using frameworks such as the "Mission, Vision, and Values" framework, organisations can develop a clear and concise statement that reflects their purpose and values. A well-crafted mission statement can serve as a guide for decision-making and can provide a sense of direction and identity for the organisation.

Establishing Business Goals and Objectives

Once an organisation has created its mission statement and values, the next step in defining its business strategy is to set specific goals and objectives. Goals and objectives provide a clear and measurable target for the organisation to aim towards, and help to ensure that everyone in the organisation is aligned towards achieving the same outcomes (Kotler & Keller, 2016).

The SMART framework is a popular approach to setting effective business goals and objectives. This framework suggests that goals should be Specific, Measurable, Achievable, Relevant, and Time-bound (Locke & Latham, 2002). Using the SMART framework helps organisations to set goals that are clear, focused, and achievable.

Specific: Goals should be clear and well-defined, with a specific outcome in mind. This helps to ensure that everyone in the organisation understands what needs to be accomplished and why.

Measurable: Goals should be quantifiable and measurable, so that progress can be tracked over time. This helps organisations to identify whether they are making progress towards their goals and to adjust their strategies as needed.

Achievable: Goals should be realistic and attainable given the organisation's resources and abilities. This helps to ensure that goals are challenging but not impossible, and that they can be accomplished with the resources available.

Relevant: Goals should be aligned with the organisation's mission, values, and overall strategy. This helps to ensure that the goals are relevant and meaningful to the organisation and its stakeholders.

Time-bound: Goals should have a clear timeline for completion. This helps to create a sense of urgency and accountability, and helps organisations to stay on track towards achieving their goals.

For example, a SMART business goal might be to increase sales revenue by 10% over the next 12 months. This goal is specific (increasing sales revenue), measurable (by 10%), achievable (with the organisation's resources and capabilities), relevant (aligned with the organisation's mission and values), and time-bound (over the next 12 months).

It's important to include stakeholders from all over the organisation in the goal-setting process to make sure that goals and objectives are in line with the organisation's mission and values. This could include employees, customers, and other key stakeholders who have a vested interest in the success of the organisation (Kotler & Keller, 2016).

Setting business goals and objectives is important, but it's also important to keep track of and evaluate progress towards these goals on a regular basis. This involves tracking key performance indicators (KPIs) that are relevant to the goals and objectives, and making adjustments as needed to ensure that the organisation stays on track (Kotler & Keller, 2016).

Establishing business goals and objectives is a critical step in defining your business strategy. Using the SMART framework helps organisations to set clear, focused, and achievable goals that are well-aligned with their mission and values. By involving stakeholders in the goal-setting process and regularly monitoring progress towards these goals, organisations can stay on track towards achieving their desired outcomes.

Crafting a Business Strategy

Creating a business strategy means making a plan for how to reach the goals and objectives of the business. Porter (1996) says that a well-written business strategy helps to guide decision-making, allocate resources, and make sure that all of the organisation's efforts are focused on achieving its goals.

To craft a business strategy, it is important to start by analysing the organisation's external and internal environment. This includes doing a SWOT analysis (Strengths, Weaknesses, Opportunities, and Threats) to figure out the organisation's strengths and weaknesses, as well as the opportunities and threats it faces (Kotler & Keller, 2016). By understanding the external and internal environment, organisations can identify potential areas of competitive advantage and develop a strategy that leverages these advantages.

One key framework for developing a business strategy is Porter's Generic Strategies framework. This framework outlines three generic strategies that organisations can use to achieve competitive advantage: cost leadership, differentiation, and focus (Porter, 1985).

Cost Leadership: Companies that use a cost leadership strategy try to make their products or services as cheap as possible in their industry. This allows them to offer products or services at a lower price than their competitors, while still maintaining profitability.

Differentiation: Businesses that use differentiation as a strategy try to make their products or services stand out from those of their competitors. This lets them stand out based on things like the quality of their products, how they look, or how well they treat their customers.

Focus: A focus strategy is used by businesses that want to serve a specific niche in their industry. This allows them to tailor their products or services to the unique needs and preferences of their target market, and to differentiate themselves based on their specialised expertise or knowledge.

Once an organisation has identified its competitive strategy, it is important to develop a set of tactics or initiatives that will help to achieve its goals and objectives. This may include developing new products or services, expanding into new markets, improving operational efficiency, or investing in new technology or infrastructure (Kotler & Keller, 2016).

Creating a business strategy means making a plan for how to reach the goals and objectives of the business. By analysing the external and internal environment, organisations can identify potential areas of competitive advantage and develop a strategy that leverages these advantages. The Porter's Generic Strategies framework provides a useful framework for developing a competitive strategy, while the tactics or initiatives should be tailored to the organisation's unique needs and resources.

iv. Porter's Generic Strategy

Overview of Porter's Generic Strategy

Michael Porter created the Porter's Generic Strategy framework to assist organisations in determining and pursuing a competitive strategy that will give them a long-term advantage in their sector. The framework describes three general strategies that organisations can use to gain a competitive edge: cost leadership, differentiation, and focus (Porter, 1985).

Cost Leadership

Cost leadership is a business strategy in which a company tries to make its production or delivery costs the lowest in its industry. This allows them to offer products or services at a lower price than their competitors, while still maintaining profitability. Organisations that pursue a cost leadership strategy must focus on operational efficiency, economies of scale, and cost control to be successful.

Differentiation

Differentiation is a business strategy in which a company tries to make its products or services stand out from those of its competitors. This lets them stand out based on things like the quality of their products, how they look, or how well they treat their customers. To be successful, organisations that try to stand out must focus on innovation, creativity, and building their brand.

Focus

Focus is a business strategy where companies try to fill a certain need in their industry. This allows them to tailor their products or services to the unique needs and preferences of their target market, and to differentiate themselves based on their specialised expertise or knowledge. Organisations that pursue a focus strategy must have a deep understanding of their target market and be able to deliver products or services that meet their specific needs.

The Porter's Generic Strategy framework provides a useful tool for organisations to identify their competitive strategy and to develop a plan of action for achieving their goals and objectives. By understanding the advantages and challenges of each strategy, organisations can make an informed decision about which strategy is best suited for their unique circumstances and resources.

Porter's Generic Strategy is a framework that describes three generic strategies that organisations can use to gain a competitive advantage: cost leadership, differentiation, and focus. Each strategy has its own pros and cons, and when choosing a strategy, organisations need to think carefully about their unique needs and resources. The Porter's Generic Strategy framework provides a useful tool for organisations to identify their competitive strategy and to develop a plan of action for achieving their goals and objectives.

Cost Leadership Strategy

The cost leadership strategy is one of the three generic strategies outlined in Porter's Generic Strategy framework (Porter, 1985). The cost leadership strategy involves achieving the lowest cost of production or delivery within an industry. Organisations that pursue a cost leadership strategy aim to offer products or services at a lower price than their competitors, while still maintaining profitability (Kotler & Keller, 2016).

Organisations must focus on operational efficiency, economies of scale, and cost control if they want their cost leadership strategy to work. This means that the organisation as a whole needs to put a lot of effort into lowering costs, including in areas like purchasing, production, logistics, and distribution (Porter, 1985). Also, organisations need to put money into technology and processes that help them be more cost-effective and run more efficiently over time.

One advantage of the cost leadership strategy is that it allows organisations to offer products or services at a lower price than their competitors, which can be a significant competitive advantage in price-sensitive markets. In addition, the focus on cost reduction can help organisations to improve their overall profitability and financial performance (Kotler & Keller, 2016).

However, the cost leadership strategy also has its challenges. To be successful, organisations must be able to achieve a sustainable cost advantage over their competitors. This requires ongoing investment in technology and process improvement, as well as a focus on innovation to find new ways to reduce costs (Porter, 1985). In

43

addition, the focus on cost reduction may lead to a lack of investment in other areas, such as product quality or customer service, which could harm the organisation's long-term competitiveness.

The cost leadership strategy is a generic strategy that involves achieving the lowest cost of production or delivery within an industry. Organisations that pursue a cost leadership strategy aim to offer products or services at a lower price than their competitors, while still maintaining profitability. To be successful with this strategy, organisations must focus on operational efficiency, economies of scale, and cost control. While the cost leadership strategy has its advantages, organisations must also be aware of the challenges and trade-offs involved in pursuing this strategy.

Differentiation Strategy

The differentiation strategy is one of the three generic strategies outlined in Porter's Generic Strategy framework (Porter, 1985). The differentiation strategy involves offering products or services that are unique or distinct from those offered by competitors. Organisations that pursue a differentiation strategy aim to differentiate themselves based on factors such as product quality, design, or customer service (Kotler & Keller, 2016).

Organisations must focus on innovation, creativity, and building their brand if they want their differentiation strategy to work. Porter (1985) says that this needs a strong focus on research and development and a willingness to invest in product design, marketing, and customer service. In addition, organisations must be able to clearly communicate the unique value proposition of their products or services to customers, in order to differentiate themselves effectively.

One benefit of the differentiation strategy is that it lets businesses offer products or services that are hard for competitors to copy. This can give them a big edge in the market. In addition, customers may be willing to pay a premium price for products or services that are perceived as unique or high quality (Kotler & Keller, 2016).

However, the differentiation strategy also has its challenges. To be successful, organisations must be able to sustain their differentiation over time and continue to innovate and improve their products or services. In addition, the focus on differentiation may lead to higher production or delivery costs, which could impact profitability (Porter, 1985).

Differentiation is a general strategy that means offering products or services that are different from what competitors offer. Organisations that use a differentiation strategy try to stand out by doing things like making better products, having better designs, or giving better customer service. To be successful with this strategy, organisations must focus on innovation, creativity, and brand building, and be able to sustain their differentiation over time. While the differentiation strategy has its advantages, organisations must also be aware of the challenges and trade-offs involved in pursuing this strategy.

Focus Strategy

The focus strategy is one of the three generic strategies outlined in Porter's Generic Strategy framework (Porter, 1985). The focus strategy involves serving a specific niche or segment within an industry, rather than targeting the broader market. Organisations that pursue a focus strategy aim to tailor their products or services to the unique needs and preferences of their target market (Kotler & Keller, 2016).

To be successful with a focus strategy, organisations must have a deep understanding of their target market and be able to deliver products or services that meet their specific needs. This requires a strong focus on market research, as well as the ability to be agile and adapt quickly to changes in the market (Porter, 1985). In addition, organisations must be able to differentiate themselves based on their specialised expertise or knowledge in the target market.

One benefit of the focus strategy is that it lets businesses gain a strong competitive edge in their target market. Kotler and Keller (2016) say that companies can stand out from their competitors and build strong customer loyalty by making their products and services fit the unique needs of their customers.

However, the focus strategy also has its challenges. To be successful, organisations must be able to sustain their differentiation over time and continue to meet the evolving needs of their target market. In addition, the focus on a specific niche or segment may limit opportunities for growth or expansion into other markets (Porter, 1985).

The focus strategy is an industry-wide plan that involves serving a specific niche or segment. Focused organisations try to make sure that their products or services meet the specific needs and wants of their target market. To be successful with this strategy, organisations must have a deep understanding of their target market and be able to differentiate themselves based on their specialised expertise or knowledge. While the focus strategy has its advantages, organisations must also be aware of the challenges and trade-offs involved in pursuing this strategy.

Development of Porter's Generic Strategy

Michael Porter's Generic Strategy framework outlines three generic strategies that organisations can use to achieve competitive advantage: cost leadership, differentiation, and focus (Porter, 1985). However, Porter later expanded the framework to include two additional strategies: focus differentiation and best cost provider (Porter, 1998).

Focus Differentiation

The focus-difference strategy is a hybrid strategy that combines the focus strategy and the differentiation strategy. Businesses that use this strategy try to meet the needs of a specific market niche or industry segment while also offering goods or services that are different from those of competitors (Porter, 1998). This allows them to differentiate themselves based on factors such as product quality, design, or customer service, and to tailor their offerings to the specific needs of their target market.

To be successful with this strategy, organisations must have a deep understanding of their target market and be able to deliver products or services that meet their specific needs. This requires a strong focus on market research, innovation, and agility (Porter, 1998). Additionally, organisations must be able to sustain their differentiation over time and continue to meet the evolving needs of their target market.

Best Cost Provider

The cost leadership strategy and the differentiation strategy are both parts of the best cost provider strategy. Organisations that pursue this strategy aim to achieve the lowest cost of production or delivery within their industry while also offering products or services that are of a higher quality than those offered by competitors (Porter, 1998). This allows them to differentiate themselves based on both price and

49

quality and to offer a value proposition that is attractive to a broad range of customers.

To be successful with this strategy, organisations must focus on operational efficiency, economies of scale, and cost control, while also investing in innovation, research and development, and brand building (Porter, 1998). Additionally, organisations must be able to achieve a sustainable cost advantage over their competitors while still maintaining product or service quality.

The Porter's Generic Strategy framework describes five generic strategies that organisations can use to gain a competitive edge: cost leadership, differentiation, focus, focus differentiation, and best cost provider. Each strategy needs a different set of skills and resources, so when an organisation chooses a strategy, it needs to think carefully about its own circumstances and resources.

v. Strategic Planning and Implementation

Strategic planning and implementation is a critical aspect of business management strategy. It involves the process of developing a comprehensive plan that outlines an organisation's goals and objectives, as well as the strategies and tactics required to achieve them (David, 2017). The strategic planning process typically involves several steps that can be further expanded:

> ➢ Environmental Analysis: The first step in strategic planning is to do an analysis of the outside and inside factors that could affect how well an organisation does. This could mean looking at things like the political, economic, social, technological, and legal environment (PESTLE analysis) and

the competitive environment (Porter's Five Forces analysis) (David, 2017).

➢ SWOT Analysis: The next step is to do a SWOT analysis, which is an evaluation of an organisation's strengths, weaknesses, opportunities, and threats. This helps organisations to identify areas where they can capitalise on their strengths, address their weaknesses, take advantage of opportunities, and mitigate threats (David, 2017).

➢ Goal Setting: Once an organisation has conducted its environmental and SWOT analysis, it can set its goals and objectives. These goals should be specific, measurable, achievable, relevant, and time-bound (SMART) (Kotler & Keller, 2016).

➢ Strategy Development: Once an organisation has set goals and objectives, it can make plans to reach them. The organisation's mission, vision, and values, as well as its goals and objectives, should be in line with these strategies. When making their strategies, organisations must take into account their unique skills, resources, and limits (David, 2017).

➢ Planning for implementation: Once the strategies are made, the next step is to make a plan for implementation that shows what needs to be done to reach the goals and objectives. The implementation plan should have a timeline, specific steps to take, how resources will be used, and ways to measure how well the plan is working (David, 2017).

➢ Kotler and Keller (2016) say that an organisation needs strong leadership, good communication, and teamwork in order to put a strategic plan into action. (David, 2017) Organisations must also make sure that their employees understand the plan and how their individual roles help the organisation reach its goals and objectives.

Also, organisations need to keep track of and evaluate their progress often to make sure they are on track to reach their goals (David, 2017). This could mean measuring and analysing data on performance, doing regular reviews and assessments, and changing the strategic plan as needed.

Overall, planning and carrying out a strategic plan is a complicated and ongoing process that needs careful thought and attention to detail. Organisations can set themselves up for long-term success and a competitive edge by making and implementing a strong strategic plan.

Creating a Strategic Plan

A strategic plan is a road map that shows an organisation's long-term goals, strategies, and tactics (David, 2017). Creating a strategic plan involves a series of steps that help organisations to identify their strengths, weaknesses, opportunities, and threats, and to develop strategies that leverage their strengths and mitigate their weaknesses (Kotler & Keller, 2016).

The following are some key steps involved in creating a strategic plan:

1. Do an Analysis of the Environment: The first step in making a strategic plan is to do an analysis of the environment to find the internal and external factors that could affect how well an organisation does. This could mean looking at things like the political, economic, social, technological, and legal environment (PESTLE analysis) and the competitive environment (Porter's Five Forces analysis) (David, 2017).

2. Conduct a SWOT Analysis: The next step is to conduct a SWOT analysis to identify the organisation's strengths, weaknesses, opportunities, and threats. This helps

organisations to identify areas where they can capitalise on their strengths, address their weaknesses, take advantage of opportunities, and mitigate threats (David, 2017).

3. Set Goals and Objectives: Once the environmental and SWOT analysis is complete, the next step is to set goals and objectives. These goals should be specific, measurable, achievable, relevant, and time-bound (SMART) (Kotler & Keller, 2016).

4. Make plans: Once organisations have set goals and objectives, they can make plans for how to reach them. The organisation's mission, vision, and values, as well as its goals and objectives, should be in line with these strategies. When making their strategies, organisations must take into account their unique skills, resources, and limits (David, 2017).

5. Implementation Plan: Make a plan for putting the strategies into action. Once the strategies are made, the next step is to make a plan for putting them into action. This plan should list the steps that need to be taken to reach the goals and objectives. The implementation plan should include a timeline, specific actions, resource allocation, and performance measures (David, 2017).

6. Communicate the Plan: Once the strategic plan is made, it is important to communicate it well to all stakeholders, such as employees, customers, investors, and partners (Kotler & Keller, 2016). Clear communication makes sure that everyone knows what the plan is and how they can help it work.

7. Monitor and Evaluate Progress: Finally, it's important to keep an eye on and evaluate the strategic plan's progress on a regular basis to make sure the organisation is on track to reach its goals and objectives. This could mean measuring and analysing performance data, doing regular reviews and assessments, and making changes to the strategic plan as needed (David, 2017).

Creating a strategic plan involves a series of steps that help organisations to identify their strengths, weaknesses, opportunities, and threats, and to develop strategies that leverage their strengths and mitigate their weaknesses. By creating and implementing a strong strategic plan, organisations can position themselves for long-term success and competitive advantage.

Implementing Your Strategy

Implementing a strategic plan is a critical aspect of business management strategy. Effective implementation requires strong leadership, communication, and collaboration within the organisation (Kotler & Keller, 2016). The following are some key steps involved in implementing your strategy:

1. Create an Action Plan: The first step in putting your strategy into action is to create an action plan that shows the specific steps that need to be taken to reach the goals and objectives of the strategic plan. The action plan should have a timeline, specific steps to take, a way to allocate resources, and ways to measure performance (David, 2017).

2. Communicate the Plan: Once the action plan is made, it is important to communicate it well to all stakeholders, such as employees, customers, investors, and partners (Kotler & Keller, 2016). Clear communication makes sure that everyone knows what the plan is and how they can help it work.

3. Align the Organisation: Implementing a strategic plan requires alignment of the entire organisation to the plan's

objectives. Employees must understand their individual roles and responsibilities, and how they contribute to the overall success of the organisation (David, 2017). To ensure alignment, organisations may need to adjust their structure, systems, and processes to support the strategic plan.

4. Allocate Resources: Putting a strategic plan into action takes the right amount of money, people, and technology (Kotler & Keller, 2016). Organisations must ensure that they allocate resources effectively to support the plan's objectives.

5. Monitor Progress: It's important to regularly check on progress and evaluate performance to make sure the organisation is on track to reach its goals and objectives. This could mean measuring and analysing performance data, doing regular reviews and assessments, and making changes to the strategic plan as needed (David, 2017).

6. Adjust and Adapt: Finally, organisations must be able to adjust and adapt their strategies as needed. External factors such as changes in the market or the competitive landscape may require organisations to revise their strategies to remain competitive (Kotler & Keller, 2016).

To put a strategic plan into action, you need to take a number of steps, such as making an action plan, sharing the plan, getting the organisation on the same page, allocating resources, keeping track of progress, and changing and adapting the plan as needed. By effectively implementing their strategic plans, organisations can position themselves for long-term success and competitive advantage.

Measuring and Evaluating Progress

Measuring and evaluating progress is an essential aspect of implementing a strategic plan. By regularly monitoring performance data and evaluating progress, organisations can ensure that they are on track to achieve their goals and objectives, and make adjustments to their strategic plan as needed (David, 2017).

The following are some key steps involved in measuring and evaluating progress:

1. Set Performance Measures: The first step in measuring and evaluating progress is to set performance measures. Kotler and Keller (2016) say that performance measures should be in line with the strategic plan's goals and objectives and

should be specific, measurable, achievable, relevant, and time-bound (SMART).

2. Collect Data: Once performance measures are established, organisations must collect data to measure progress. This may involve collecting data from a variety of sources, including financial statements, customer surveys, employee feedback, and market research (David, 2017).

3. Analyse Data: Once organisations have collected data, they need to look at it to learn more about how well they are doing. Kotler and Keller (2016) say that one way to do this is to compare actual performance to what was planned, find trends, and figure out how internal and external factors affect performance.

4. Review and Evaluate Progress: Once organisations have analysed performance data, they can review and evaluate progress. This may involve conducting regular reviews and assessments of performance, identifying areas of success, and areas that need improvement (David, 2017).

5. Make Adjustments: Finally, based on the review and assessment of progress, organisations may need to make adjustments to their strategic plan. Kotler and Keller (2016) say that this could mean changing goals and objectives,

strategies, resources, or processes and systems to improve performance.

Measuring and evaluating progress is a critical aspect of implementing a strategic plan. By setting performance measures, collecting data, analysing data, reviewing and assessing progress, and making adjustments as needed, organisations can ensure that they are on track to achieve their goals and objectives, and position themselves for long-term success and competitive advantage.

vi. Innovation and Entrepreneurship

Innovation and entrepreneurship are critical elements of business management strategy. This chapter explores the role of innovation and entrepreneurship in achieving long-term success and competitive advantage, and how organisations can foster innovation and develop an entrepreneurial mindset to achieve their goals.

➢ Fostering Innovation in Your Organisation: To encourage innovation in your organisation, it's important to understand the different types of innovation, the innovation process, and the benefits and challenges of innovation (Schaper, Volery, Weber, & Gibson, 2014). Organisations can develop an innovation strategy that aligns with their overall business strategy, identifying and prioritising innovation opportunities, creating a culture of innovation, and establishing a supportive organisational structure for innovation.

➢ Developing an Entrepreneurial Mindset: Developing an entrepreneurial mindset involves cultivating the characteristics of successful entrepreneurs, such as creativity, risk-taking, and persistence. (Schaper, Volery, Weber, & Gibson, 2014) Organisations can encourage people to think like entrepreneurs by making an environment that supports entrepreneurship, coming up with a clear business model and value proposition, and getting funding and other resources for new ventures.

➢ Encouraging People to Take Risks and Try New Things: A key part of innovation and entrepreneurship is encouraging people to take risks and try new things. Organisations can encourage people to take risks and try new things by creating a culture that values trying new things, learning from mistakes, and always getting better. This means coming up with good processes for innovation and entrepreneurship, dealing with risk and uncertainty, and giving employees the freedom to take calculated risks (Schaper, Volery, Weber, & Gibson, 2014).

This chapter explores the concepts of innovation and entrepreneurship and their role in business management strategy. By fostering innovation in your organisation, developing an entrepreneurial mindset, and encouraging risk-taking and experimentation, organisations can establish a culture of innovation and create new products, services, and ventures that can help them achieve long-term success and competitive advantage.

Fostering Innovation in Your Organisation

Innovation is crucial for organisations to remain competitive and achieve long-term success. To foster innovation in your organisation, it is important to understand the different types of innovation, the innovation process, and the benefits and challenges of innovation (Schaper, Volery, Weber, & Gibson, 2014).

Developing an Innovation Strategy

Organisations can develop an innovation strategy that aligns with their overall business strategy. This involves identifying and prioritising innovation opportunities, creating a culture of innovation, and establishing a supportive organisational structure for innovation. Organisations can also develop an innovation portfolio that includes incremental, breakthrough, and disruptive innovations (Kotler & Keller, 2016).

Creating a Culture of Innovation

Creating a culture of innovation involves encouraging experimentation, risk-taking, and continuous learning. This involves establishing an open and collaborative work environment that supports creativity and idea generation. Organisations can also establish innovation metrics and incentives to encourage innovation and track progress (Kotler & Keller, 2016).

Establishing a Supportive Organisational Structure

Establishing a supportive organisational structure involves developing effective innovation processes and systems. This involves establishing an innovation team or department, creating innovation networks with external partners, and allocating resources to support innovation projects. Organisations can also use innovation tools and techniques such as design thinking, open innovation, and crowdsourcing to generate new ideas and solutions (Schaper, Volery, Weber, & Gibson, 2014).

Challenges of Fostering Innovation

Fostering innovation may pose several challenges for organisations. These challenges may include resistance to change, lack of resources, insufficient innovation culture, and inability to measure and track innovation progress. Organisations must address these challenges by developing a comprehensive innovation strategy, creating a supportive work environment, and establishing a culture of innovation (Kotler & Keller, 2016).

Fostering innovation in your organisation is critical for achieving long-term success and competitive advantage. By developing an innovation strategy, creating a culture of innovation, and establishing a supportive organisational structure, organisations can generate new ideas and solutions and remain competitive in a rapidly changing market (Schaper, Volery, Weber, & Gibson, 2014).

Developing an Entrepreneurial Mindset

People and organisations that want to be creative and start new businesses need to have an entrepreneurial mindset. Schapper, Volery, Weber, and Gibson (2014) say that having an entrepreneurial mindset means developing traits like creativity, willingness to take risks, and persistence.

Characteristics of Successful Entrepreneurs

Successful entrepreneurs share certain characteristics that set them apart from others. These characteristics include creativity, risk-taking, proactivity, passion, and persistence (Schaper, Volery, Weber, & Gibson, 2014). Creativity involves generating new ideas and solutions, while risk-taking involves making calculated decisions and taking action despite uncertainty. Proactivity involves taking initiative and being proactive in pursuing opportunities, while passion involves having a strong sense of purpose and commitment to achieving goals. Persistence involves overcoming obstacles and persevering in the face of adversity.

Encouraging an Entrepreneurial Mindset

Organisations can encourage an entrepreneurial mindset by creating a supportive environment for entrepreneurship. This involves establishing an organisational culture that values creativity, risk-taking, and innovation. Organisations can also provide training and development opportunities for employees to enhance their entrepreneurial skills and mindset (Schaper, Volery, Weber, & Gibson, 2014).

Developing a Clear Business Model and Value Proposition

People and organisations that want to start and run a new business must come up with a clear business model and value proposition. This means finding a need in the market, making a product or service that fills that need, and coming up with a business model that makes it possible to sell that product or service. Organisations can also use tools such as the business model canvas to map out their business model and value proposition (Osterwalder & Pigneur, 2010).

Securing Funding and Other Resources

Securing funding and other resources is another important aspect of developing an entrepreneurial mindset. Organisations can seek funding from various sources such as venture capitalists, angel investors, crowdfunding, and government grants. Additionally, organisations can seek support from incubators, accelerators, and other entrepreneurial support organisations that provide resources and mentorship to help new ventures succeed (Schaper, Volery, Weber, & Gibson, 2014).

People and organisations that want to be creative and start new businesses need to have an entrepreneurial mindset. People and organisations can start and run successful new businesses by developing the traits of successful entrepreneurs, making a clear business model and value proposition, and getting funding and other resources.

Encouraging Risk-Taking and Experimentation

A key part of developing an entrepreneurial mindset and encouraging innovation in organisations is to encourage people to take risks and try new things. Schaper, Volery, Weber, and Gibson (2014) found that organisations that encourage experimentation and are willing to take risks are more likely to be innovative and able to respond to changes in the market.

Creating a Culture of Experimentation

Creating a culture of experimentation involves establishing an environment where employees feel encouraged to try new ideas and approaches. Organisations can encourage experimentation by recognising and rewarding creativity, celebrating failures as opportunities for learning, and providing resources and support for innovation projects (Amabile & Khaire, 2008).

Learning from Failure

Learning from failure is a critical aspect of encouraging risk-taking and experimentation. Organisations that view failures as opportunities for learning tend to be more innovative and adaptable. To learn from failure, organisations can conduct post-mortems or debriefs to understand what went wrong and how to improve, and encourage employees to share their failures and lessons learned with others (Edmondson, 2011).

Empowering Employees

To encourage employees to try new things and take calculated risks, it's also important to give them the freedom to do so. (Amabile & Khaire, 2008) Organisations can give employees power by giving them autonomy and decision-making power, giving them ownership over their work, and giving them the resources and support they need to put their ideas into action.

Managing Risk and Uncertainty

Managing risk and uncertainty is a key challenge in encouraging risk-taking and experimentation. Organisations must balance the need for innovation with the need for financial stability and risk management. To manage risk and uncertainty, organisations can use risk management techniques such as scenario planning, establish clear decision-making processes, and seek feedback from stakeholders and customers (Schaper, Volery, Weber, & Gibson, 2014).

Getting people to take risks and try new things is a key part of developing an entrepreneurial mindset and making organisations more innovative. Organisations can encourage innovation and flexibility in a market that changes quickly by creating a culture of trying new things, learning from mistakes, giving employees more power, and managing risk and uncertainty.

vii. Strategic Marketing and Sales

Strategic marketing and sales are critical components of business management strategy. This chapter explores the role of marketing and sales in achieving business objectives, the different marketing and sales strategies, and how to develop and implement effective marketing and sales plans.

Marketing Strategies

Target markets, a value proposition, and marketing mix elements, such as product, price, promotion, and place, are all parts of a marketing strategy. Kotler and Keller (2016) say that different marketing strategies, such as segmentation, targeting, positioning, and differentiation, can help businesses reach their marketing goals.

Sales Strategies

Finding potential customers, making a sales process, and setting sales goals and metrics are all part of a sales strategy. Organisations can use various sales strategies such as consultative selling, relationship selling, and solution selling to achieve their sales objectives (Spiro, Stanton, & Rich, 2008).

Developing a Marketing and Sales Plan

To make a marketing and sales plan, you have to figure out what your business goals are, look at the market and the competition, and come up with marketing and sales strategies and tactics. Organisations can use various tools and frameworks such as SWOT analysis, Porter's five forces model, and the marketing mix to develop an effective marketing and sales plan (Kotler & Keller, 2016).

Implementing a Marketing and Sales Plan

Implementing a marketing and sales plan means putting marketing and sales strategies into action, keeping track of how well they work, and making changes as needed. Organisations can use various marketing and sales tools and techniques such as digital marketing, social media marketing, and customer relationship management to implement their marketing and sales plan (Spiro, Stanton, & Rich, 2008).

Strategic marketing and sales are critical components of business management strategy. By developing and implementing effective marketing and sales plans, organisations can achieve their business objectives, reach their target markets, and gain a competitive advantage in the market.

Understanding Your Customers and Target Market

An important part of making a good marketing and sales plan is knowing your customers and target market. By understanding the needs and wants of your target customers, you can develop products and services that meet their needs, and create marketing messages and sales strategies that resonate with them.

Market Segmentation

Market segmentation is the process of breaking up a large market into smaller groups of customers with similar needs and traits. Kotler and Keller (2016) say that organisations can find different parts of their target market by using criteria like demographics, psychographics, and behaviour. By dividing the market into segments, businesses can make sure that their marketing and sales plans meet the needs and preferences of each segment.

Targeting

Targeting means picking one or more parts of the market to focus on based on how much money they could make and how much they could grow. Organisations can use various targeting strategies such as undifferentiated targeting, differentiated targeting, and concentrated targeting to focus on their target market (Kotler & Keller, 2016). By targeting specific segments of the market, organisations can create marketing messages and sales strategies that are more relevant and compelling to those customers.

Customer Research

Customer research involves gathering information about customers' needs, preferences, and behaviours. Organisations can use various research methods such as surveys, focus groups, and interviews to gather customer insights. By conducting customer research,

75

organisations can gain a deeper understanding of their target customers and develop products and services that meet their needs (Kotler & Keller, 2016).

Competitive Analysis

Competitive analysis involves identifying and analysing competitors in the market. Organisations can use various tools and techniques such as SWOT analysis and Porter's five forces model to assess the competitive landscape and identify opportunities and threats (Kotler & Keller, 2016). By conducting competitive analysis, organisations can develop marketing and sales strategies that differentiate them from their competitors and gain a competitive advantage.

Understanding your customers and target market is a crucial aspect of developing an effective marketing and sales plan. By dividing the market into segments, focusing on certain segments, doing customer research, and looking at the competition, businesses can come up with marketing and sales plans that meet the needs of their target customers and give them an edge in the market.

Developing a Marketing Strategy

To make a marketing strategy, you have to figure out who your target market is, come up with a value proposition, and figure out the product, price, promotion, and place. A well-developed marketing strategy can help organisations to reach their target customers, differentiate themselves from their competitors, and achieve their marketing objectives.

Identifying the Target Market

To find the target market, you have to figure out which group of people is most likely to be interested in the product or service. This can be done through market segmentation, which divides a larger market into smaller groups of consumers who have similar needs and characteristics (Kotler & Keller, 2016). By figuring out who the target market is, businesses can make sure their marketing messages and sales strategies are more relevant and appealing to those customers.

Creating a Value Proposition

Creating a value proposition means coming up with a unique selling proposition that tells the target customers about the unique benefits and value of the product or service. The value proposition should be clear, concise, and focused on the customer's needs and wants (Osterwalder & Pigneur, 2010). By coming up with a strong value proposition, a business can set itself apart from its competitors and attract and keep customers.

Developing the Marketing Mix Elements

Developing the marketing mix elements involves developing strategies for product, price, promotion, and place. Organisations can use various tools and techniques such as product positioning, pricing strategies, advertising, and distribution channels to develop an effective marketing mix (Kotler & Keller, 2016). By developing a strong marketing mix, organisations can create a cohesive and effective marketing plan that achieves their marketing objectives.

Implementing and Monitoring the Marketing Strategy

Implementing and keeping an eye on the marketing strategy means putting the marketing plan into action and keeping an eye on how well it works. Organisations can use various tools and techniques such as customer feedback, sales metrics, and market research to monitor performance and make adjustments as needed (Kotler & Keller, 2016). By monitoring the marketing strategy, organisations can ensure that the marketing plan is effective and adjust the plan as needed to achieve their marketing objectives.

To make a marketing strategy, you have to figure out who your target market is, come up with a value proposition, and figure out the product, price, promotion, and place. Organisations can reach their target customers, stand out from their competitors, and reach their marketing goals by coming up with a good marketing strategy.

Building a Sales Strategy

Finding potential customers, making a sales process, and setting sales goals and metrics are all parts of building a sales strategy. An effective sales strategy can help organisations to reach their target customers, increase sales revenue, and achieve their sales objectives.

Identifying Potential Customers

Identifying potential customers involves determining the group of individuals or organisations who are most likely to purchase the product or service being offered. This can be done through customer segmentation, which divides a larger market into smaller groups of customers who have similar needs and characteristics (Spiro, Stanton, & Rich, 2008). By identifying potential customers, organisations can develop sales messages and strategies that are more relevant and compelling to those customers.

Creating a Sales Process

Creating a sales process means coming up with a step-by-step plan for how to find potential customers, get in touch with them, and turn them into paying customers. (Spiro, Stanton, and Rich, 2008) The sales process should be made to be quick, effective, and focused on the customer. By making a sales process, companies can make sure that the sales team has all the tools and resources it needs to sell the product or service well.

Establishing Sales Goals and Metrics

Setting sales goals and metrics means setting goals for sales revenue, customer acquisition, and other key performance indicators. Organisations can use various metrics such as sales revenue, conversion rates, and customer retention rates to measure the effectiveness of their sales strategy (Spiro, Stanton, & Rich, 2008). By establishing sales goals and metrics, organisations can ensure that the sales team is aligned with the overall business objectives and is working towards achieving them.

Implementing and Monitoring the Sales Strategy

Implementing and monitoring the sales strategy involves executing the sales plan and monitoring performance to determine its effectiveness. Organisations can use various tools and techniques such as sales reports, customer feedback, and market research to monitor performance and make adjustments as needed (Spiro, Stanton, & Rich, 2008). By monitoring the sales strategy, organisations can ensure that the sales plan is effective and adjust the plan as needed to achieve their sales objectives.

Finding potential customers, making a sales process, and setting sales goals and metrics are all parts of building a sales strategy. By making a good sales strategy, businesses can reach their target customers, make more money from sales, and reach their sales goals.

viii. Strategic Human Resource Management

Strategic Human Resource Management (SHRM) is the process of aligning the human resource function with the strategic objectives of the organisation. SHRM involves designing and implementing HR policies and practices that support the overall business strategy and help the organisation to achieve its goals (Armstrong & Taylor, 2014). A well-designed SHRM system can help organisations to attract and retain top talent, develop the skills and capabilities of employees, and improve overall organisational performance.

The Strategic Role of HR

HR's strategic role is to work with top management to create and put into place HR policies and practises that support the business's overall strategy. HR professionals can play a critical role in ensuring that the organisation has the talent, skills, and capabilities needed to achieve its strategic objectives (Armstrong & Taylor, 2014). By aligning HR policies and practices with the overall business strategy,

HR can help to improve organisational performance and create a competitive advantage.

Recruiting and Selecting Employees

Finding and choosing employees means finding and attracting people with the skills, knowledge, and experience needed to help the organisation reach its strategic goals. HR professionals can use various recruitment and selection methods such as job advertisements, employee referrals, and interviews to identify and select top talent (Armstrong & Taylor, 2014). By recruiting and selecting top talent, organisations can build a high-performance workforce that is aligned with the overall business strategy.

Training and Development

Training and development are about making sure that employees have the skills, knowledge, and abilities they need to do their jobs well and help the organisation reach its strategic goals. HR professionals can use various training and development methods such as on-the-job training, coaching, and mentoring to develop the skills and capabilities of employees (Armstrong & Taylor, 2014). By investing in training and development, organisations can build a highly skilled and motivated workforce that is aligned with the overall business strategy.

Performance Management

Setting goals and objectives for employees' performance, giving them feedback on their performance, and rewarding or punishing them based on their performance are all parts of performance management. HR professionals can use various performance management methods such as performance appraisals, 360-degree feedback, and performance-based incentives to manage employee performance (Armstrong & Taylor, 2014). By implementing a performance management system, organisations can improve employee productivity, motivation, and overall organisational performance.

Strategic Human Resource Management (SHRM) is the process of aligning the human resource function with the strategic objectives of the organisation. SHRM involves designing and implementing HR policies and practices that support the overall business strategy and help the organisation to achieve its goals. By aligning HR policies and practices with the overall business strategy, organisations can attract and retain top talent, develop the skills and capabilities of employees, and improve overall organisational performance.

Recruiting and Hiring Top Talent

Recruiting and hiring top talent is a critical component of Strategic Human Resource Management (SHRM). Hiring top talent involves identifying and attracting candidates who have the skills, knowledge, and experience needed to achieve the strategic objectives of the organisation (Armstrong & Taylor, 2014). By hiring top talent, organisations can build a high-performance workforce that is aligned with the overall business strategy.

Identifying Top Talent

To find the best people, you need to know what knowledge, skills, and experience are needed for each job and write a job description that lists these needs. HR professionals can find top talent in a number of ways, including job ads, employee recommendations, and social media (Armstrong & Taylor, 2014). By figuring out who the best people are, organisations can make sure they hire the best people for the job.

Assessing Candidates

To evaluate candidates, you have to compare their knowledge, skills, and experience to what the job needs. HR professionals can use various assessment methods, such as interviews, tests, and assessments centres, to evaluate candidates (Armstrong & Taylor, 2014). By assessing candidates, organisations can ensure that they are selecting the most qualified candidate for the position.

Attracting Top Talent

To get the best people, you need to have a good employer brand that makes people want to work for you. HR professionals can attract top talent in a number of ways, such as by offering competitive salaries and benefits, giving employees chances to grow in their careers, and making the workplace a pleasant place to be (Armstrong & Taylor, 2014). By attracting the best people, organisations can make sure they can hire the best people for the job.

Recruiting and hiring top talent is a critical component of Strategic Human Resource Management (SHRM). Hiring top talent involves identifying and attracting candidates who have the skills, knowledge, and experience needed to achieve the strategic objectives of the organisation. By hiring top talent, organisations can build a high-performance workforce that is aligned with the overall business strategy.

Developing and Managing Your Workforce

Developing and managing your workforce is an important aspect of Strategic Human Resource Management (SHRM). It involves designing and implementing HR policies and practices that support the development and retention of the organisation's workforce. By developing and managing the workforce, organisations can ensure that they have the talent, skills, and capabilities needed to achieve their strategic objectives (Armstrong & Taylor, 2014).

Training and Development

Training and development are about making sure that employees have the skills, knowledge, and abilities they need to do their jobs well and help the organisation reach its strategic goals. HR professionals can use various training and development methods such as on-the-job training, coaching, and mentoring to develop the skills and capabilities of employees (Armstrong & Taylor, 2014). By investing in training and development, organisations can build a highly skilled and motivated workforce that is aligned with the overall business strategy.

Performance Management

Setting goals and objectives for employees' performance, giving them feedback on their performance, and rewarding or punishing them based on their performance are all parts of performance management. HR professionals can use various performance management methods such as performance appraisals, 360-degree feedback, and performance-based incentives to manage employee performance (Armstrong & Taylor, 2014). By implementing a performance management system, organisations can improve employee productivity, motivation, and overall organisational performance.

Retention Strategies

Retention strategies involve making and putting into place HR policies and practises that help the organisation keep its best employees. HR professionals can use various retention strategies such as offering competitive salaries and benefits, providing opportunities for career development, and creating a positive work environment (Armstrong & Taylor, 2014). By implementing retention strategies, organisations can ensure that they are able to retain their top talent and build a high-performance workforce that is aligned with the overall business strategy.

Succession Planning

Succession planning is the process of finding and training employees who could fill key leadership roles in the organisation. (Armstrong & Taylor, 2014) HR professionals can prepare employees for leadership positions in a number of ways, such as through leadership development programs, mentoring, and job rotation. By putting in place a succession planning system, organisations can make sure they have the right people with the right skills to fill key leadership positions.

Developing and managing your workforce is an important aspect of Strategic Human Resource Management (SHRM). It involves designing and implementing HR policies and practices that support the development and retention of the organisation's workforce. By developing and managing the workforce, organisations can ensure that they have the talent, skills, and capabilities needed to achieve their strategic objectives.

Aligning HR Strategy with Business Strategy

One of the key objectives of Strategic Human Resource Management (SHRM) is to align HR strategy with business strategy. This involves designing and implementing HR policies and practices that support the achievement of the organisation's strategic objectives (Armstrong & Taylor, 2014). By aligning HR strategy with business strategy, organisations can ensure that their HR function is contributing to the overall success of the organisation.

Understanding Business Strategy

The first step in aligning HR strategy with business strategy is to understand the organisation's business strategy. To do this, you need to know the organisation's mission, vision, strategic goals, and competitive environment (Armstrong & Taylor, 2014). By understanding the business strategy of the organisation, HR professionals can create and implement HR policies and practises that help the organisation reach its strategic goals.

Designing HR Policies and Practices

Once HR professionals understand the business strategy of an organisation, they can create and implement HR policies and practises that help the organisation reach its strategic goals. (Armstrong & Taylor, 2014) This could mean coming up with policies and procedures for hiring and firing, training and development, performance management, pay and benefits, and so on. By designing HR policies and practices that are aligned with the organisation's business strategy, HR professionals can ensure that the HR function is contributing to the overall success of the organisation.

Implementing HR Policies and Practices

After HR professionals make policies and practises that are in line with the business strategy of the organisation, they have to put them into action. This means telling the employees about the policies and practices, training them on the policies and practices, and keeping an eye on how well the policies and practises are working (Armstrong & Taylor, 2014). HR professionals can make sure that the HR function is contributing to the success of the organisation as a whole by putting in place HR policies and practises that are in line with the business strategy of the organisation.

Measuring the Effectiveness of HR Strategy

After HR policies and practises have been made and put into place, it's important to measure how well they work. This means keeping an eye on how well the HR function is doing and how HR policies and practises affect the organisation's ability to reach its strategic goals (Armstrong & Taylor, 2014). By measuring the effectiveness of HR strategy, HR professionals can identify areas for improvement and make adjustments to the HR policies and practices as needed.

Aligning HR strategy with business strategy is a critical component of Strategic Human Resource Management (SHRM). It involves designing and implementing HR policies and practices that support the achievement of the organisation's strategic objectives. By aligning HR strategy with business strategy, organisations can ensure that their HR function is contributing to the overall success of the organisation.

ix. Financial Management and Planning

Financial management and planning are critical components of strategic business management. This chapter focuses on the importance of financial management and planning in achieving business objectives, and the key financial concepts and techniques that can be used to manage financial resources effectively.

Financial Management

Financial management is the efficient and effective use of money to help a business reach its goals. It includes managing cash flow, budgeting, financial reporting, and financial analysis (Brigham & Ehrhardt, 2013). Financial management helps organisations to make informed decisions about investments, financing, and operations, and to monitor and control their financial performance.

Financial Planning

Financial planning involves setting financial goals and objectives, and developing a plan to achieve them. It includes forecasting future financial performance, budgeting, and developing financial strategies (Brigham & Ehrhardt, 2013). Financial planning helps organisations to allocate financial resources effectively, and to manage financial risks and uncertainties.

Financial Concepts and Techniques

This chapter talks about important financial ideas and methods that can be used to manage money well. These include financial statements, financial ratios, time value of money, capital budgeting, and cost of capital (Brigham & Ehrhardt, 2013). These concepts and techniques are important for making informed financial decisions and for monitoring and controlling financial performance.

Financial management and planning are critical components of strategic business management. Financial management involves the efficient and effective management of financial resources to achieve business objectives, while financial planning involves setting financial goals and objectives, and developing a plan to achieve them. This chapter covers key financial concepts and techniques that can be used to manage financial resources effectively, including financial statements, financial ratios, time value of money, capital budgeting, and cost of capital.

Understanding Financial Statements

Financial statements are a key tool for understanding an organisation's financial performance and position. Financial statements provide important information about an organisation's revenue, expenses, assets, liabilities, and equity. This section will discuss the three main financial statements: the income statement, the balance sheet, and the cash flow statement.

- ➢ Income Statement: The income statement, also known as the profit and loss statement, shows an organisation's revenue and expenses over a specific period of time, typically a month or a year. The income statement provides important information about an organisation's profitability, and is used by investors and creditors to evaluate an organisation's financial performance (Wild, Shaw, & Chiappetta, 2015).

➢ Balance Sheet: The balance sheet shows an organisation's assets, liabilities, and equity at a specific point in time. The balance sheet provides important information about an organisation's financial position, and is used by investors and creditors to evaluate an organisation's financial stability and liquidity (Wild, Shaw, & Chiappetta, 2015).

➢ Cash Flow Statement: The cash flow statement shows an organisation's inflows and outflows of cash over a specific period of time. The cash flow statement provides important information about an organisation's liquidity and cash management, and is used by investors and creditors to evaluate an organisation's ability to generate cash and meet its financial obligations (Wild, Shaw, & Chiappetta, 2015).

➢ Financial ratio analysis is the process of judging a company's financial performance and position by looking at its financial ratios. Financial ratios are used to compare an organisation's financial performance and position to industry averages, historical performance, or competitors (Wild, Shaw, & Chiappetta, 2015). Common financial ratios include profitability ratios, liquidity ratios, and solvency ratios.

Financial statements provide important information about an organisation's financial performance and position. The income statement shows an organisation's revenue and expenses over a specific period of time, the balance sheet shows an organisation's assets, liabilities, and equity at a specific point in time, and the cash flow statement shows an organisation's inflows and outflows of cash over a specific period of time. Financial ratio analysis involves using financial ratios to evaluate an organisation's financial performance and position.

Managing Cash Flow and Budgeting

Cash flow management and budgeting are important for any organisation to be financially stable and successful. Cash flow management is the process of keeping track of and managing the money coming in and going out of an organisation to make sure it has enough money to pay its bills. Budgeting involves setting financial goals and developing a plan to achieve them. This section will discuss the importance of cash flow management and budgeting, and some key strategies for effective cash flow management and budgeting.

Importance of Cash Flow Management

Cash flow management is important to make sure that a business has enough money to pay its bills, like paying its suppliers, employees, and creditors. Poor cash flow management can lead to financial distress and even bankruptcy (Kimmel, Weygandt, & Kieso, 2019). Cash flow management means keeping track of how much money comes in and goes out, predicting how much money will come in and go out in the future, and managing cash reserves.

Key Strategies for Effective Cash Flow Management

To effectively manage cash flow, organisations can employ the following strategies:

1. Establishing a cash reserve: Establishing a cash reserve can help an organisation to weather unexpected financial challenges, such as a downturn in the economy or a disruption in the supply chain. A cash reserve should be established by setting aside a certain percentage of revenue each month or quarter.

2. Managing accounts receivable: Managing accounts receivable involves monitoring and collecting payments

from customers in a timely manner. This can help to improve cash flow and reduce the risk of bad debts. Organisations can also offer discounts for early payment or consider using invoice financing as a way to manage accounts receivable.

3. Managing accounts payable means keeping track of payments to suppliers and making sure they get paid on time. This can help to improve cash flow and reduce the risk of late payment penalties. Organisations can negotiate longer payment terms with suppliers or consider using supply chain financing as a way to manage accounts payable.

Importance of Budgeting

Budgeting is critical for setting financial goals and developing a plan to achieve them. Budgets can help organisations to allocate financial resources effectively, prioritise spending, and monitor and control financial performance (Kimmel, Weygandt, & Kieso, 2019).

Key Strategies for Effective Budgeting

To effectively manage budgets, organisations can employ the following strategies:

1. Setting realistic financial goals: Setting realistic financial goals can help to ensure that budgets are achievable and aligned with the organisation's strategic objectives. Goals should be specific, measurable, achievable, relevant, and time-bound (SMART).

2. Controlling and keeping an eye on spending: Controlling and keeping an eye on spending can help make sure that budgets are kept and that resources are used well. This can be achieved through regular reporting and analysis of financial data.

3. Updating budgets regularly: Updating budgets regularly can help to ensure that budgets are responsive to changes in the business environment, such as changes in the economy or changes in the competitive landscape. Budgets should be reviewed and updated at least annually, but may need to be updated more frequently in dynamic business environments.

Effective cash flow management and budgeting are critical for achieving financial stability and success in any organisation. To manage cash flow effectively, organisations should establish a cash reserve, manage accounts receivable and accounts payable, and maintain a strong focus on cash management. To manage budgets effectively, organisations should set realistic financial goals, monitor and control spending, and update budgets regularly.

Financing Your Business

Getting enough money to grow and develop is one of the most difficult things for a business to do. There are different ways to finance a business, such as through debt financing, equity financing, and other sources. This section will discuss the importance of financing, and some key strategies for securing financing for your business.

Importance of Financing

Businesses need money to invest in new products, grow their operations, and move into new markets. (Brigham & Ehrhardt, 2016) says that not having enough money can cause businesses to miss out on opportunities, do poorly, or even fail. Effective financing means coming up with a financial strategy that fits with the goals and objectives of the organisation.

Key Strategies for Securing Financing

To secure financing for your business, consider the following strategies:

Develop a Business Plan

A business plan is a detailed document that lists the organisation's goals, objectives, and financial projections. It shows how the organisation will grow and change, and lenders and investors need to see it in order to give money. (Barney & Hesterly, 2019) A well-written business plan can also show investors that the organisation knows the market, the competition, the risks, and the opportunities. A business plan should include a description of the organisation's products or services, market analysis, financial projections, and management team.

Explore Debt Financing Options

Debt financing involves borrowing money from lenders, such as banks or credit unions, and repaying the loan over time with interest. This can be a good way to get money, but it also means taking on debt and making payments on a regular basis. Before asking for a loan, businesses should make sure they have a good credit history and a good plan for paying it back (Brigham & Ehrhardt, 2016).

Lenders may also look at the organisation's cash flow, its collateral, and its ability to pay back the loan.

Explore Equity Financing Options

Equity financing involves selling shares in the organisation to investors in exchange for capital. This can be an effective way to raise funds without taking on debt, but it also involves giving up a portion of ownership and control of the organisation. Equity financing can be a viable option for businesses that have a high growth potential and are willing to give up some control in exchange for capital (McKaskill, 2019). Organisations should carefully evaluate potential investors to ensure that they have a shared vision and can bring value beyond the capital infusion.

Consider Alternative Financing Sources

Alternative ways to get money, like crowdfunding, peer-to-peer lending, and microloans, can be a good choice for small businesses that can't get traditional loans. You can get money through these options even if you don't have a lot of assets or a good credit history (Ratten, 2018). But organisations should think carefully about the costs and risks of these options and make sure they have a good plan for paying back the money.

Financing is critical for businesses to invest in growth and development. Effective financing involves developing a financial strategy that aligns with the organisation's goals and objectives, and exploring various financing options, including debt financing, equity financing, and alternative financing sources.

x. Operations and Supply Chain Management

Operations and supply chain management involve designing, planning, and controlling the processes and resources that are needed to make and deliver goods and services. This section will discuss the importance of operations and supply chain management, and some key strategies for managing these critical functions.

Importance of Operations and Supply Chain Management

Effective operations and supply chain management is essential for ensuring that products and services are delivered to customers in a timely, cost-effective, and high-quality manner. Poor operations and supply chain management can result in inefficiencies, delays, and increased costs, which can negatively impact customer satisfaction and profitability (Jacobs & Chase, 2017). Effective operations and supply chain management involves developing strategies that align with the organisation's goals and objectives and involves managing resources such as people, materials, and equipment.

Key Strategies for Managing Operations and Supply Chain

To manage operations and supply chain effectively, consider the following strategies:

- ➢ Develop a Production Plan: A production plan is a map that shows the organisation's production goals, timelines, and resource needs. (Chopra & Meindl, 2015) A well-thought-out production plan can help to make sure that production goes smoothly and quickly, reducing the chance of delays or bottlenecks. A production plan should consider factors such as capacity, demand, and inventory levels.

- ➢ Implement Quality Control: Quality control means making sure that products and services meet or exceed customer expectations by creating processes and procedures. (Slack, Brandon-Jones, and Johnston, 2019) say that good quality control can make customers happier, cut down on waste, and make things run more smoothly. Setting quality standards, keeping an eye on and measuring performance, and putting in place processes for continuous improvement should all be part of quality control.

➤ Optimise the Supply Chain: Supply chain Optimisation means coming up with processes and strategies that make sure materials, products, and information flow smoothly from suppliers to customers (Monczka, Handfield, Giunipero, & Patterson, 2015). This can mean building relationships with suppliers, keeping track of inventory levels, and putting in place technologies for the supply chain.

➤ Adopt lean principles. Lean principles involve making processes and plans that get rid of waste and make things run more smoothly. Womack, Jones, and Roos (1990) say that this can be done with strategies like just-in-time production, continuous improvement, and total quality management. Lean principles can help organisations to improve productivity, reduce costs, and increase customer satisfaction.

Effective operations and supply chain management is critical for ensuring that products and services are delivered to customers in a timely, cost-effective, and high-quality manner. Managing these functions involves developing strategies that align with the organisation's goals and objectives and managing resources such as people, materials, and equipment.

Streamlining Your Operations

Streamlining your operations means finding and getting rid of the parts of your business that aren't working well so you can increase productivity, cut costs, and make customers happier. This section will discuss some key strategies for streamlining your operations.

Key Strategies for Streamlining Your Operations

 - ➢ Do a Business Process Analysis: A business process analysis involves making a diagram of the steps in each of your business processes, figuring out where the bottlenecks are, and looking for ways to make your business more efficient (Davenport, 2013). This can help you to identify areas where improvements can be made to streamline your operations and improve productivity.
 - ➢ Automate Processes: Automating processes can help to reduce the time and resources required to complete tasks, improve accuracy, and enhance efficiency. This can involve

implementing technologies such as enterprise resource planning (ERP) systems, customer relationship management (CRM) software, and supply chain management (SCM) tools (Monk & Wagner, 2018). Automating processes can help to reduce the risk of errors and delays, enabling organisations to operate more efficiently.

➢ Implement Lean Principles: Using lean principles means finding waste in your business processes and getting rid of it. Womack, Jones, and Roos (1990) say that this can be done with strategies like just-in-time production, continuous improvement, and total quality management. Lean principles can help organisations to improve productivity, reduce costs, and increase customer satisfaction.

➢ Develop a Culture of Continuous Improvement: Creating a culture of continuous improvement means creating a place where employees are encouraged to find and suggest ways to make business processes better. (Liker & Convis, 2011) Some ways to do this are through employee training, feedback systems, and recognition programs. A culture of continuous improvement can help to encourage new ideas, increase efficiency, and make customers happier.

Streamlining your operations is critical for improving productivity, reducing costs, and enhancing customer satisfaction. Key strategies for streamlining your operations include conducting a business process analysis, automating processes, implementing lean principles, and developing a culture of continuous improvement.

Managing Your Supply Chain

Managing your supply chain means making sure that information, materials, and products move smoothly from your suppliers to your customers. Effective supply chain management can help to reduce costs, improve efficiency, and enhance customer satisfaction. This section will discuss some key strategies for managing your supply chain.

Key Strategies for Managing Your Supply Chain

> ➤ Develop Good Relationships with Suppliers: Cousins, Lawson, and Squire (2008) say that having good relationships with suppliers can help improve communication, boost collaboration, and lower the risk of supply chain disruptions. This can be done by putting in

place strategies like supplier scorecards, regular meetings with suppliers, and planning sessions with them.

➢ Optimise Inventory Levels: To optimise inventory levels, you need to find the right balance between having enough stock to meet demand and keeping too much stock. Monczka, Handfield, Giunipero, and Patterson (2015) say that one way to do this is to use strategies like "just-in-time" production, inventory management systems, and shorter lead times. Optimising inventory levels can help to reduce costs and improve efficiency.

➢ Implement Supply Chain Technologies: Implementing supply chain technologies can help to improve communication, visibility, and efficiency in the supply chain. This can involve implementing technologies such as radio-frequency identification (RFID) tags, global positioning systems (GPS), and electronic data interchange (EDI) (Christopher, 2016). Implementing supply chain technologies can help to reduce the risk of errors and delays, enabling organisations to operate more efficiently.

➢ Monitor Performance: Monitoring supply chain performance involves measuring and analysing supply chain metrics such as on-time delivery, order fulfilment, and inventory turnover.

112

This can help organisations to identify areas where improvements can be made and to benchmark their performance against industry standards (Cousins, Lawson, & Squire, 2008). Monitoring performance can help to drive continuous improvement in the supply chain.

Managing your supply chain is important if you want to cut costs, increase efficiency, and make customers happier. Key ways to manage your supply chain are to build strong relationships with your suppliers, make sure you have the right amount of inventory, use supply chain technologies, and keep an eye on performance.

Improving Efficiency and Productivity

Improving efficiency and productivity involves maximising output while minimising input. This can help to reduce costs, increase revenue, and enhance customer satisfaction. This section will discuss some key strategies for improving efficiency and productivity.

Key Strategies for Improving Efficiency and Productivity

➢ Implement Lean Principles: Using lean principles means finding waste in your business processes and getting rid of it. Womack, Jones, and Roos (1990) say that this can be done with strategies like just-in-time production, continuous improvement, and total quality management. Lean principles can help organisations to improve productivity, reduce costs, and increase customer satisfaction.

➢ Automate Processes: Automating processes can help to reduce the time and resources required to complete tasks, improve accuracy, and enhance efficiency. This can involve implementing technologies such as enterprise resource planning (ERP) systems, customer relationship management (CRM) software, and supply chain management (SCM) tools (Monk & Wagner, 2018). Automating processes can help to reduce the risk of errors and delays, enabling organisations to operate more efficiently.

➢ Setting goals, measuring performance, and giving feedback to employees are all parts of putting performance management systems into place. This can help to motivate employees, enhance accountability, and improve productivity (Armstrong & Taylor, 2014). Performance management systems can also help organisations to identify areas where improvements can be made.

> Continuous Improvement: Continuous improvement means finding ways to make business processes better and making small changes to them over time. (Liker & Convis, 2011) Some ways to do this are through employee training, feedback systems, and recognition programs. A culture of continuous improvement can help to encourage new ideas, increase efficiency, and make customers happier.

Improving efficiency and productivity is a must if you want to cut costs, make more money, and make your customers happier. Key strategies for improving efficiency and productivity include implementing lean principles, automating processes, implementing performance management systems, and continuous improvement.

xi. Strategic Leadership and Management

Strategic leadership and management are about setting the organisation's direction and leading it to reach its goals. Strategic leadership and management that works well can help an organisation do better, be more innovative, and be more competitive. This section will discuss some key strategies for strategic leadership and management.

> ➢ Visionary Leadership: (Kotter, 1990) Visionary leadership means making a compelling picture of the future and inspiring and motivating people to work towards that picture. A visionary leader is able to communicate the organisation's purpose, values, and goals to employees, and provide them with the resources and support they need to achieve those goals. Visionary leadership can help to foster a sense of

purpose and direction, and to promote innovation and creativity.

➢ Strategic Planning: Strategic planning involves developing a long-term plan for achieving the organisation's goals. This can involve conducting a SWOT analysis, identifying key performance indicators, and developing action plans to achieve those goals (Bryson, 2018). Strategic planning can help to align the organisation's activities with its goals and to identify and mitigate potential risks. It can also help to ensure that resources are allocated effectively and efficiently.

➢ Performance Management: Setting goals, measuring performance, and giving feedback to employees are all parts of performance management (Armstrong & Taylor, 2014). This can help to motivate employees, enhance accountability, and improve productivity. Performance management can also help organisations to identify areas where improvements can be made. It involves a continuous process of setting goals, monitoring progress, and providing feedback to employees, and can help to ensure that employees are aligned with the organisation's goals.

➢ Talent Management: (Collings, Scullion, and Vaiman, 2018) Talent management is the process of finding and developing

117

an organisation's best performers. This can be done through things like leadership development programs, training for employees, and planning for the next generation of leaders. Talent management can help to ensure that the organisation has the right people in the right positions, and to promote a culture of continuous learning and improvement. It can also help to retain high-performing employees and to develop a pool of potential leaders for the future.

➢ Change Management: Change management involves planning and implementing changes within the organisation (Kotter, 1996). This can involve changes to processes, systems, or culture. Effective change management requires a clear understanding of the reasons for change, a well-defined plan for implementing the change, and effective communication and stakeholder engagement. Change management can help organisations to adapt to changing market conditions, to improve efficiency and productivity, and to foster innovation.

Strategic leadership and management are important if an organisation wants to reach its goals, encourage new ideas, and become more competitive. Visionary leadership, strategic planning,

118

performance management, talent management, and change management are all important parts of strategic leadership and management.

Leading and Managing Change

Change is inevitable in today's dynamic business environment. Organisations must continuously adapt to changing market conditions, technologies, and customer needs to remain competitive. Leading and managing change effectively can help organisations to minimise disruption and maximise the benefits of change. This section will discuss some key strategies for leading and managing change.

Key Strategies for Leading and Managing Change

> Establish a Sense of Urgency: To start and keep a change going, leaders must make stakeholders feel like time is running out. This can be done by explaining why change is needed, what will happen if nothing is done, and what the benefits of change are (Kotter, 1996). Establishing a sense of

urgency can help to mobilise support for change and to overcome resistance. Leaders can use various techniques to create a sense of urgency, such as conducting a SWOT analysis or highlighting external threats and opportunities (Kotter, 1996).

➢ Create a Vision for Change: For change to work, you need to have a clear and compelling picture of the future. Leaders must articulate the desired end-state and communicate it to stakeholders (Kotter, 1996). The vision should be specific, measurable, and achievable, and should align with the organisation's mission and values. Leaders can involve stakeholders in developing the vision to increase ownership and commitment (Kotter, 1996).

➢ Communicate and Engage: Communication and engagement are critical for successful change. Leaders must communicate the vision for change, the rationale for change, and the expected outcomes to stakeholders (Kotter, 1996). They must also engage stakeholders in the change process, soliciting feedback and addressing concerns. Leaders can use various communication channels, such as town hall meetings, newsletters, and social media, to reach different stakeholder groups (Kotter, 1996).

➤ Empower Action: Leaders must empower stakeholders to take action to support change. This can involve providing resources, training, and support, and delegating authority to stakeholders (Kotter, 1996). Empowering action can help to build momentum and to sustain change. Leaders can also provide incentives and recognition to encourage and reward desired behaviours (Kotter, 1996).

➤ Create Short-term Wins: Creating short-term wins can help to build momentum and to reinforce the benefits of change. Leaders must identify and celebrate early successes, and communicate them to stakeholders (Kotter, 1996). Short-term wins can help to overcome resistance and to build support for change. Leaders can set achievable milestones and targets to create a sense of progress and accomplishment (Kotter, 1996).

➤ Consolidate Gains and Make More Change: Once leaders have won in the short term, they need to consolidate gains and make more changes. This can involve integrating the changes into the organisation's culture and processes, and identifying and implementing additional changes (Kotter, 1996). Consolidating gains can help to reinforce the benefits of change and to create a foundation for future change.

Leaders can also use feedback and evaluation to identify areas for improvement and to guide future change efforts (Kotter, 1996).

Leading and managing change is a critical skill for organisations to adapt to changing market conditions and to remain competitive. By following the key strategies of establishing a sense of urgency, creating a vision for change, communicating and engaging stakeholders, empowering action, creating short-term wins, and consolidating gains and producing more change, leaders can increase the likelihood of successful change implementation.

Building a High-Performing Team

By increasing productivity, innovation, and employee engagement, a team that works well can give an organisation a competitive edge. Building and maintaining a high-performing team requires a range of skills and strategies. This section will discuss some key strategies for building a high-performing team.

Key Strategies for Building a High-Performing Team

➤ Define Roles and Responsibilities: Making roles and responsibilities clear can help keep a team from getting confused or fighting with each other. Leaders must ensure that team members have a clear understanding of their roles, and how they fit into the overall team structure (Kozlowski & Bell, 2003). This can involve creating job descriptions, setting performance expectations, and providing feedback on performance.

➤ Foster Collaboration and Communication: Collaboration and communication are critical for team performance. Leaders must create a culture of open communication and encourage team members to share ideas, feedback, and concerns (Kozlowski & Bell, 2003). This can involve regular team meetings, brainstorming sessions, and team-building activities.

➤ Build Trust and Respect: Trust and respect are foundational elements of a high-performing team. Leaders must demonstrate trust and respect for team members, and encourage team members to do the same (Kozlowski & Bell, 2003). This can involve creating a safe and supportive work environment, recognising and rewarding good performance, and addressing conflicts in a constructive manner.

➢ Develop Team Skills and Competencies: Developing team skills and competencies can help to improve team performance. Leaders must identify the skills and competencies needed for team success, and provide training and development opportunities (Kozlowski & Bell, 2003). This can involve cross-training, mentoring, coaching, and skills-building workshops.

➢ Set Goals and Provide Feedback: Setting goals and providing feedback can help to align team efforts and improve performance. Leaders must set clear, specific, and measurable goals for the team, and provide regular feedback on progress (Kozlowski & Bell, 2003). This can involve using performance metrics, conducting regular performance reviews, and recognising and rewarding good performance.

➢ Embrace diversity and inclusion: make everyone feel welcome. Accepting diversity and making everyone feel welcome can help a team do better by bringing in different ideas and points of view. Leaders must create a culture of inclusion, and encourage team members to value and leverage diversity (Kozlowski & Bell, 2003). This can involve providing diversity training, promoting diversity in recruitment and selection, and celebrating diverse perspectives and achievements.

Building a high-performing team requires a range of skills and strategies. Key strategies for building a high-performing team include defining roles and responsibilities, fostering collaboration and communication, building trust and respect, developing team skills and competencies, setting goals and providing feedback, and embracing diversity and inclusion. By following these strategies, leaders can build and maintain a high-performing team that can provide a competitive advantage for the organisation.

Developing Your Leadership Skills

Leadership skills are essential for success in any organisation. Developing and honing leadership skills can help individuals to become effective leaders, improve team performance, and achieve organisational goals. This section will discuss some key strategies for developing leadership skills.

Key Strategies for Developing Leadership Skills

➤ Seek Feedback: Seeking feedback can help leaders to identify areas for improvement and to gain insights into how others perceive their leadership style (Avolio & Hannah, 2008). Leaders can seek feedback from a range of sources, such as colleagues, subordinates, and mentors. Feedback can be obtained through formal methods, such as 360-degree feedback, or informal methods, such as regular check-ins.

➤ Set Learning Goals: Setting learning goals can help leaders to focus their development efforts and to measure progress (Avolio & Hannah, 2008). Leaders can identify areas in which they want to improve, such as communication skills or conflict resolution, and set specific, measurable, and achievable goals. Leaders can then develop action plans to achieve these goals, such as attending training sessions or seeking mentorship.

➤ Seek Learning Opportunities: Seeking learning opportunities can help leaders to acquire new knowledge, skills, and perspectives (Avolio & Hannah, 2008). Leaders can seek learning opportunities through various channels, such as training programs, conferences, and workshops. Leaders can also seek informal learning opportunities, such as reading books or articles, or networking with other leaders.

➢ Practice Reflection: Reflection can help leaders to gain insights into their own leadership style, and to identify areas for improvement (Avolio & Hannah, 2008). Leaders can reflect on their experiences, successes, and challenges, and identify what they have learned. Reflection can be done through various methods, such as journaling, debriefing with colleagues, or seeking feedback from others.

➢ Build Relationships: Building relationships can help leaders to develop their interpersonal skills and to build a support network (Avolio & Hannah, 2008). Leaders can build relationships with colleagues, subordinates, and mentors, and seek opportunities to collaborate and learn from others. Building relationships can also help leaders to establish trust and credibility with others.

➢ Lead by Example: Leading by example can help leaders to model the behaviours and attitudes that they expect from others (Avolio & Hannah, 2008). Leaders can demonstrate integrity, accountability, and a commitment to excellence. Leading by example can also help to build trust and respect among team members.

Developing leadership skills is essential for success in any organisation. Key strategies for developing leadership skills include seeking feedback, setting learning goals, seeking learning opportunities, practicing reflection, building relationships, and leading by example. By following these strategies, individuals can become effective leaders and achieve their personal and organisational goals.

xii. Real World Strategic Management

Quick Case Study: Tesla

Tesla is a great example of how effective business management strategies can be aligned with market trends, customer needs, and organisational capabilities to achieve long-term growth and success. Tesla's business management strategy can be analysed through various strategic management frameworks and models.

Tesla's focus on the customer is in line with market analysis, which is a key part of strategic management. Tesla's electric cars are made to meet customers' needs and preferences, and the company has built a strong brand identity that appeals to people who care about the environment. This focus on the customer has led to a loyal customer base that spreads the word about Tesla's products (Porter, 2008).

Tesla's emphasis on innovation and entrepreneurship aligns with the principles of Porter's generic strategies model. The company has differentiated itself from competitors through its advanced battery technology, which has revolutionised the electric car industry by enabling longer driving ranges and faster charging times. Additionally, Tesla's solar panels and energy storage solutions are designed to integrate with each other, creating a more sustainable energy ecosystem. Tesla's focus on innovation has helped it to maintain a competitive advantage and stay ahead of the competition (Porter, 1996).

Tesla's strategic leadership and management align with the principles of transformational leadership, which emphasises innovation, risk-taking, and a willingness to challenge the status quo. Tesla's CEO, Elon Musk, is widely regarded as a visionary leader who has been instrumental in driving the company's success. Musk's leadership style has created a culture of innovation and entrepreneurship within Tesla, where employees are encouraged to take risks and develop new and disruptive technologies (Bass & Riggio, 2006).

Tesla's financial planning and management are in line with financial management principles, which is a key part of strategic management. The company has gotten money from a variety of places, such as venture capitalists, strategic investors, and government grants. This has made it possible for the company to put money into research and development, make more products, and go into new markets. Tesla's ability to manage cash flow and budget effectively has allowed it to explore financing options when necessary, ensuring its long-term financial viability (Hitt, Ireland & Hoskisson, 2016).

In conclusion, Tesla's success can be attributed to its effective business management strategy, which is in line with market trends, customer needs, and organisational capabilities. Focusing on customer-centeredness, innovation, entrepreneurship, strategic leadership and management, and financial planning and management has helped the company keep doing well in a market that is very competitive and changes quickly. So, Tesla's story of success is an example for businesses all over the world and shows how important it is to create and use good business management strategies to grow and be successful.

Quick Case Study: Apple Inc.

Apple's business management strategy aligns with several strategic management frameworks and models:

Apple's focus on innovation aligns with the principles of Porter's generic strategy model. The company has differentiated itself from competitors through its unique design and engineering capabilities, which have resulted in a range of highly innovative products and services. Apple's emphasis on innovation has enabled it to maintain a competitive advantage and stay ahead of the competition (Porter, 1996).

Apple's focus on the customer is in line with market analysis principles, which is a key part of strategic management. Apple's products and services are made to meet the needs and preferences of its customers. Because of this, Apple has a loyal customer base that spreads the word about its products. Also, the company has built a strong brand identity that consumers like, which has helped it get a big share of the market in many different product categories (Porter, 2008).

Apple's strategic leadership and management align with the principles of transformational leadership, which emphasise innovation, risk-taking, and a willingness to challenge the status quo. The company's CEO, Tim Cook, has been instrumental in driving Apple's success, following in the footsteps of the legendary founder, Steve Jobs. Cook has developed a culture of innovation within Apple, where employees are encouraged to take risks and develop new and disruptive technologies (Bass & Riggio, 2006).

Apple's financial planning and management are in line with financial management principles, which is a key part of strategic management. The company has a lot of cash on hand, which lets it put a lot of money into research and development, make more products, and enter new markets. Additionally, Apple has maintained a strong financial position, allowing it to explore financing options when necessary, ensuring its long-term financial viability (Hitt, Ireland & Hoskisson, 2016).

In conclusion, Apple's business management strategy aligns with several strategic management frameworks and models, including Porter's generic strategy model, market analysis, transformational leadership, and financial management. Apple's focus on innovation, customer-centricity, strategic leadership and management, and financial management has enabled it to achieve sustained success in a highly competitive and rapidly changing market, solidifying its position as one of the world's leading technology companies.

Quick Case Study: Amazon

Amazon's business management strategy aligns with several strategic management frameworks and models:

Amazon's focus on cost leadership aligns with the principles of Porter's generic strategy model. The company has built a robust logistics infrastructure and implemented cost-saving measures, enabling it to offer low prices on a wide range of products. This has enabled Amazon to become a dominant player in the online retail market, attracting price-sensitive customers and undercutting traditional brick-and-mortar retailers (Porter, 1980).

Second, Amazon's focus on the customer is in line with market analysis principles, which is a key part of strategic management. Amazon has a reputation for having great customer service, a huge selection of products, and shipping that is quick and reliable. This has helped the company build a base of loyal customers, bring in new ones, and increase the number of customers who stay with the company (Porter, 1985).

Amazon's strategic leadership and management align with the principles of transformational leadership, which emphasise innovation, risk-taking, and a willingness to challenge the status quo. Amazon's CEO, Jeff Bezos, has been instrumental in driving the company's success, focusing on long-term growth and innovation. Bezos has developed a culture of experimentation within Amazon, where employees are encouraged to take risks and develop new and disruptive technologies (Bass & Riggio, 2006).

Amazon's financial planning and management are in line with financial management principles, which is an important part of strategic management. The company has put a lot of money into research and development, growth, and acquisitions, which has helped it offer a wider range of products and services and move into new markets. Additionally, Amazon has maintained a strong financial position, allowing it to explore financing options when necessary, ensuring its long-term financial viability (Hitt, Ireland & Hoskisson, 2016).

In conclusion, Amazon's business management strategy aligns with several strategic management frameworks and models, including Porter's generic strategy model, market analysis, transformational leadership, and financial management. Amazon's focus on cost leadership, customer-centricity, strategic leadership and management, and financial management has enabled it to achieve sustained success in a highly competitive and rapidly changing market, solidifying its position as one of the world's leading e-commerce and technology companies.

Quick Case Study: NIKE

Nike's business management strategy aligns with several strategic management frameworks and models:

Nike's differentiation strategy aligns with the principles of Porter's generic strategies model. The company has consistently focused on developing innovative products, leveraging its strong brand identity, and creating a unique customer experience. Nike has achieved this through its focus on research and development, product design, and marketing, enabling it to differentiate itself from competitors and increase brand loyalty (Porter, 1980).

Nike's customer-centric approach aligns with the principles of market analysis, which is a critical component of strategic management. Nike has a strong focus on understanding the needs and preferences of its target market and creating products that meet those needs. This has enabled the company to develop a loyal customer base, attract new customers, and increase customer retention rates (Porter, 1985).

Nike's strategic leadership and management align with the principles of transformational leadership. Nike's CEO, John Donahoe, has been instrumental in driving the company's success, focusing on innovation, sustainability, and social responsibility. Donahoe has encouraged collaboration, experimentation, and risk-taking, leading to the development of new products and services and the company's focus on sustainability and social responsibility (Bass & Riggio, 2006).

Nike's financial planning and management are in line with financial management principles, which are a key part of strategic management. The company has kept its finances in good shape by putting an emphasis on cash reserves and managing debt. Additionally, Nike has invested heavily in research and development, marketing, and sponsorship deals, enabling it to diversify its product and service offerings and enter new markets (Hitt, Ireland & Hoskisson, 2016).

In conclusion, Nike's business management strategy aligns with several strategic management frameworks and models, including Porter's generic strategies model, market analysis, transformational leadership, and financial management. Nike's focus on differentiation, customer-centricity, strategic leadership and management, and financial management has enabled it to achieve sustained success in a highly competitive and rapidly changing market, solidifying its position as one of the world's leading sports and lifestyle brands.

Quick Case Study: Ryanair

Ryanair's business management strategy aligns with several strategic management frameworks and models:

Ryanair's cost leadership strategy aligns with the principles of Porter's generic strategy model. The company has consistently focused on offering low-cost flights, while maintaining a high level of efficiency and profitability. Ryanair has achieved this through a number of initiatives, such as reducing non-essential services, using secondary airports, and implementing strict cost controls (Porter, 1980).

Ryanair's focus on the customer is in line with market analysis principles, which are a key part of strategic management. Ryanair puts a lot of effort into knowing what its target market wants and needs and making sure it has products and services that meet those needs. This has helped the company build a base of loyal customers, bring in new ones, and keep more of the ones it already has (Porter, 1985).

Ryanair's strategic leadership and management align with the principles of transformational leadership. Ryanair's CEO, Michael

O'Leary, has been instrumental in driving the company's success, focusing on innovation, cost reduction, and customer service. O'Leary has encouraged collaboration, experimentation, and risk-taking, leading to the development of new products and services and the company's continued growth (Bass & Riggio, 2006).

The way Ryanair manages and plans its finances is in line with the principles of financial management, which is a key part of strategic management. The company has maintained a strong financial position, with a focus on cost reduction, revenue maximisation, and strategic investments. Additionally, Ryanair has invested heavily in technology, enabling it to streamline its operations and reduce costs (Hitt, Ireland & Hoskisson, 2016).

In conclusion, Ryanair's business management strategy aligns with several strategic management frameworks and models, including Porter's generic strategy model, market analysis, transformational leadership, and financial management. Ryanair's focus on cost leadership, customer-centricity, strategic leadership and management, and financial management has enabled it to achieve sustained success in a highly competitive and dynamic industry, making it one of the largest and most profitable airlines in Europe.

Quick Case Study: Blockbuster

One example of a company that failed to implement proper strategic management is Blockbuster. Blockbuster was a video rental company that dominated the market in the 1990s and early 2000s. However, as the industry shifted towards digital streaming, Blockbuster failed to adapt and lost its market share to companies like Netflix.

Blockbuster's failure to implement proper strategic management had several consequences. Firstly, the company missed out on the opportunity to invest in new technologies, such as digital streaming, that could have allowed it to maintain its dominance in the industry. Instead, Blockbuster continued to focus on its traditional business model of physical stores and DVD rentals.

Blockbuster failed to understand the changing needs and preferences of its target market. As consumers increasingly turned to digital streaming services, Blockbuster's physical store model became outdated and unattractive to consumers. This led to declining sales, profits, and market share for the company.

Blockbuster's lack of strategic leadership and management contributed to its downfall. The company's management was slow to recognise the threat posed by digital streaming services and was reluctant to change its business model. Additionally, the company's financial management and planning were inadequate, leading to significant debt and financial losses (Kim & Mauborgne, 2004).

In the end, Blockbuster's failure to use proper strategic management had serious effects on the company. Sales, profits, and market share went down, and the company got into a lot of debt and lost a lot of money. The company went out of business because it couldn't adapt to changing market conditions and didn't have strategic leadership or management.

Quick Case Study: Kodak

An example of a company that failed to implement proper strategic management is Kodak. Kodak was a dominant player in the photography industry for decades, but its failure to keep up with digital photography and changing consumer preferences ultimately led to its downfall.

Kodak's failure to implement proper strategic management had several consequences. Firstly, the company failed to recognise the potential of digital photography and invested too heavily in its traditional film business. While Kodak did eventually develop digital photography products, it was too late, and the company had already lost significant market share to competitors such as Canon and Nikon.

Kodak's inability to adapt to changing consumer preferences also contributed to its downfall. The company had a strong brand and a loyal customer base but failed to anticipate the shift towards digital photography and mobile devices. As a result, Kodak's products became less relevant and attractive to consumers, leading to declining sales and profits.

Kodak's financial planning and management were not good enough, which led to a lot of debt and financial losses. The company was slow to respond to changes in the market and didn't cut costs or reorganise its business when it should have. This led to financial problems and, in the end, bankruptcy in 2012.

In the end, Kodak's failure to use proper strategic management had serious effects on the company. Its market share dropped, it had money problems, and it eventually went bankrupt. The company failed because it didn't see the potential of digital photography, didn't adapt to changing consumer tastes, and didn't handle its money well.

Quick Case Study: Starbucks

In the early 2000s, Starbucks' sales and profits were going down due to its rapid growth and lack of new ideas. This was primarily due to a few factors, such as the fact that the company had expanded too quickly, opening too many stores too fast and thereby diluting the quality of the coffee that it served. Additionally, many customers began to perceive Starbucks as a corporate behemoth that had lost its connection with its original values and mission.

Starbucks took a broad strategic management approach that focused on several key areas to deal with these problems. First, the company cut back on its plans to open new stores and focused on making the customer experience better in the stores it already had. This meant changing the layout of the stores to make them feel more welcoming, training the baristas to help them serve customers better, and coming up with new products and flavours to keep customers interested and coming back.

Secondly, Starbucks repositioned its brand to emphasise quality and sustainability. The company began sourcing ethically grown and produced coffee, which helped to differentiate it from its competitors and attract customers who were concerned about sustainability and social responsibility. Starbucks also launched initiatives to reduce waste and promote environmentally friendly practises, such as recycling programmes and using more eco-friendly materials in stores.

Thirdly, Starbucks embraced technology to improve its operations and enhance the customer experience. This included introducing mobile ordering and payment, which made it more convenient for customers to order and pay for their drinks, and launching a loyalty programme to incentivise repeat business.

These strategic management changes proved to be successful for Starbucks. By focusing on improving the customer experience and repositioning its brand to emphasise quality and sustainability, the company was able to regain customer trust and loyalty. Additionally, the adoption of technology helped to improve the efficiency of operations and enhance the overall customer experience, which in turn helped to drive growth and profits.

As of 2021, Starbucks will have more than 32,000 locations around the world. It is one of the most well-known and successful food and drink brands. The success of the company shows how important strategic management is for long-term success and growth in a market with a lot of competition.

Quick Case Study: Ford

"The Way Forward," Ford Motor Company's strategic management plan, was a big change from its old ways, which in the early 2000s had led to a loss of market share, more competition, and inefficient operations. With this new approach, Ford was able to figure out what was most important and make changes that helped the company grow.

The restructuring of operations to become more efficient and reduce costs was one of the critical steps Ford took. Ford was able to cut costs and make more money by closing factories, letting people go, and streamlining its supply chain. Additionally, Ford's strategic decision to focus on smaller, more fuel-efficient vehicles that responded to changing consumer preferences and stricter emissions regulations allowed it to improve its product line-up and stay ahead of the competition.

Another significant change that Ford made was investing heavily in technology and innovation to develop new products and improve the customer experience. The development of the MyFord Touch infotainment system and the launch of electric and hybrid vehicles were some of the technological innovations that Ford brought to the market, improving its brand image and customer satisfaction.

Overall, Ford's implementation of "The Way Forward" strategy proved to be successful. In 2009, Ford was the only major American automaker to avoid bankruptcy during the financial crisis, and it continued to perform well in the years that followed. By addressing its financial difficulties, improving its operations and product line-up, and investing in technology and innovation, Ford was able to thrive in a highly competitive industry.

However, it's worth noting that while Ford's strategic management changes have been successful, it is essential to keep up with evolving market trends, consumer preferences, and technological advancements to remain competitive. Therefore, continued implementation and adaptation of proper strategic management practises are critical to the long-term success of any company.

xiii. Conclusion

Business management strategy is a critical aspect of organisational success. Effective business management strategies can help organisations to achieve their goals, sustain a competitive advantage, and remain relevant in a constantly changing business environment. Developing and implementing a successful business management strategy involves several key components, including analysing the business environment, defining business goals and objectives, crafting a business strategy, implementing the strategy, and measuring and evaluating progress.

Analysing the business environment is an important first step in developing a successful business management strategy. Understanding the industry, market, and competitors can help organisations to identify opportunities and threats, and to develop strategies that leverage strengths and mitigate weaknesses. This analysis can include a review of industry trends, market size, customer needs, and competitor strategies.

For a business management strategy to work, it is also important to set clear business goals and objectives. Goals and objectives should be specific, measurable, achievable, relevant, and time-bound (SMART), and should be aligned with the overall business strategy. Once goals and objectives are defined, HR, marketing, financial, and operational strategies can be aligned to support them.

Crafting a business strategy involves developing a plan for achieving business goals and objectives. This can involve selecting a specific business model, such as cost leadership or differentiation, and determining how the organisation will create value for customers. It can also involve developing strategies for entering new markets, expanding product lines, or diversifying the business.

Implementing the business strategy involves putting the plan into action. This can involve allocating resources, developing processes and systems, and communicating the strategy to stakeholders. It is important to involve key stakeholders, such as employees and customers, in the implementation process to ensure buy-in and support.

To make sure the business management strategy works, it's important to measure and evaluate progress. Organisations should establish metrics and performance indicators to measure progress toward goals and objectives. These metrics should be regularly reviewed and adjusted as needed.

In addition to these key parts, effective business management strategies must also focus on fostering innovation, developing human resources, managing finances, and optimising operations. Innovation can help organisations to stay ahead of competitors and respond to changing customer needs. Developing human resources can help organisations to attract and retain top talent and to build a high-performing team. Managing finances is essential for maintaining financial stability and making informed business decisions. Optimising operations can help organisations to reduce costs and improve efficiency.

Leadership skills are also essential for success in business management strategy. Developing leadership skills can help individuals to become effective leaders, improve team performance, and achieve organisational goals. Key strategies for developing leadership skills include seeking feedback, setting learning goals, seeking learning opportunities, practicing reflection, building relationships, and leading by example.

Business management strategy is a critical component of organisational success. Developing and implementing an effective business management strategy involves analysing the business environment, defining business goals and objectives, crafting a business strategy, implementing the strategy, and measuring and evaluating progress. Effective business management strategies also require a focus on fostering innovation, developing human resources, managing finances, and Optimising operations. Developing leadership skills is also essential for success in business management strategy. By following these strategies, organisations can develop and implement effective business management strategies that lead to sustained competitive advantage and organisational success.

Recap of Key Points

In this book, we've talked about some of the most important parts of a successful business management strategy. These components include:

> ➤ Analysing the business environment: (Kozlowski & Bell, 2003) For effective business management strategies, you need to know the industry, market, and competitors.

> ➤ Defining business goals and objectives: (Avolio & Hannah, 2008) Clear goals and objectives that are specific, measurable, achievable, relevant, and have a time limit (SMART) can help make sure that all parts of the organisation are working together.

> ➤ Crafting a business strategy: The key to success is making a plan for how to reach business goals and objectives, such as choosing a specific business model or making plans for how to enter new markets.

> ➤ Putting the business strategy into action: Allocating resources, making processes and systems, and telling stakeholders about the strategy are all important parts of doing this well.

> ➢ Measuring and evaluating progress: It is important for the success of the business management strategy to set up metrics and performance indicators to measure progress towards goals and objectives.

In addition to these key elements, effective business management strategies must also focus on fostering innovation (Drucker, 1985), developing human resources (Collins & Smith, 2006), managing finances, and optimising operations.

Leadership skills are also essential for success in business management strategy (Kotter, 1990). Developing leadership skills can help individuals to become effective leaders, improve team performance, and achieve organisational goals. Key strategies for developing leadership skills include seeking feedback, setting learning goals, seeking learning opportunities, practicing reflection, building relationships, and leading by example.

By using these tips, organisations can come up with and use good business management strategies that give them a long-term competitive edge and help them succeed.

Future Trends in Business Management Strategy

The business world is always changing, and for a company to stay competitive, it needs to adapt to new trends and technologies. Here are five key future trends in business management strategy that are likely to shape the landscape in the coming years:

> ➤ Digital transformation: The digital transformation that is still going on is changing how businesses work and how they talk to customers. Companies need to adapt to new technologies, such as artificial intelligence, blockchain, and the Internet of Things, to stay ahead of the competition. Westerman et al. (2014) say that digital transformation is also changing how businesses interact with their customers by giving them new ways to talk and work together.

> ➤ Sustainability: As customers become more aware of environmental issues, businesses need to make their business models and products more environmentally friendly. Sustainability is becoming an important part of business strategy, from managing the supply chain to making products. Eccles and Serafeim (2013) found that companies

that put sustainability first have a better brand reputation, lower costs, and more loyal customers.

➢ Globalisation: Globalisation is transforming the way businesses operate and compete. Companies need to navigate cross-cultural differences and regulatory frameworks to succeed in diverse markets. To achieve success in global markets, companies need to develop strategies that are tailored to local conditions, while also maintaining a consistent global brand (Peng, 2014).

➢ Agile management: As companies try to be more flexible and responsive to changing customer needs and market conditions, traditional hierarchical structures are becoming less important. Self-organising teams and flexible work arrangements are two examples of agile management methods that are becoming more and more popular. (Sutherland & Schwaber, 2017) These methods let companies respond quickly to changes in the market and in customer tastes.

➢ Customer-centricity: As customers gain more power and make more demands, businesses need to put customer-centricity at the top of their business management plans. Companies that focus on creating value for customers, such

160

as personalised products and services, are more likely to succeed in the long run. To achieve customer-centricity, companies need to understand customer needs and preferences, and develop products and services that meet those needs (Osterwalder et al., 2015).

By including these future trends in business management plans, companies can stay ahead of the competition and have long-term success. By embracing digital transformation, putting sustainability first, creating global strategies, using agile management methods, and putting the customer first, companies can set themselves up for success in a business world that is always changing.

Final Thoughts and Recommendations

To make a good business management strategy, you need to think carefully about a number of things, such as the business environment, market trends, customer needs and preferences, and the organisation's strengths and weaknesses. While there is no one-size-fits-all approach to business management strategy, there are some key considerations that can help companies to develop effective strategies.

Firstly, it is important to have a deep understanding of the business environment and market trends. This means doing a thorough analysis of the industry and market, as well as figuring out who your competitors are and analysing them. By knowing how the business world works, companies can make plans that take advantage of opportunities and reduce risks.

Second, businesses should make sure they have a clear mission statement and set clear goals and objectives. This involves establishing a framework for decision-making and aligning organisational activities with strategic priorities.

Thirdly, companies need to prioritise innovation and entrepreneurship in their business management strategies. This involves fostering a culture of innovation and encouraging risk-taking and experimentation.

Fourthly, companies need to focus on developing a strong sales and marketing strategy, with a customer-centric approach that prioritises customer needs and preferences.

Fifth, companies should put strategic leadership and management at the top of their list of priorities. They should focus on building high-performing teams, leading and managing change, and getting better at being leaders.

Lastly, businesses should pay close attention to their financial management and planning, including managing cash flow and budgeting well and looking into financing options when they need to.

By keeping these things in mind, companies can come up with good business management strategies that help them reach their strategic goals and keep doing well over time.

xiv. References

Amabile, T. M., & Khaire, M. (2008). Creativity and the Role of the Leader. Harvard Business Review, 86(10), 100-109.

Ansoff, H. I. (1987). Corporate Strategy: An Analytic Approach to Business Policy for Growth and Expansion. New York: McGraw-Hill.

Armstrong, M., & Taylor, S. (2014). Armstrong's Handbook of Human Resource Management Practice. Kogan Page Publishers.

Avolio, B. J., & Hannah, S. T. (2008). Developmental readiness: Accelerating leader development. Consulting Psychology Journal: Practice and Research, 60(4), 331-347. doi: 10.1037/1065-9293.60.4.331

Baker, J. (2012). Kodak's last chance for survival. Wired Magazine. https://www.wired.com/2012/01/ff_kodak/all/

Barney, J. B., & Hesterly, W. S. (2019). Strategic Management and Competitive Advantage: Concepts and Cases. Pearson.

Bass, B. M., & Riggio, R. E. (2006). Transformational leadership (2nd ed.). Psychology Press.

Brigham, E. F., & Ehrhardt, M. C. (2016). Financial Management: Theory & Practice. Cengage Learning.

Bryson, J. M. (2018). Strategic Planning for Public and Nonprofit Organisations: A Guide to Strengthening and Sustaining Organisational Achievement. John Wiley & Sons.

Chopra, S., & Meindl, P. (2015). Supply Chain Management: Strategy, Planning, and Operation. Pearson.

Christensen, C. M. (1997). The innovator's dilemma: When new technologies cause great firms to fail. Harvard Business Review Press.

Christopher, M. (2016). Logistics & Supply Chain Management. Pearson.

Collings, D. G., Scullion, H., & Vaiman, V. (2018). Talent Management: A Critical Review. Human Resource Management Review, 28(3), 347-357.

Collins, J. C., & Porras, J. I. (1996). Building Your Company's Vision. Harvard Business Review, 74(5), 65-77.

Collins, J., & Smith, K. (2006). Entrepreneurial visions and strategic ambiguity. Organisation Science, 17(2), 170-191. doi: 10.1287/orsc.1050.0176

Cousins, P. D., Lawson, B., & Squire, B. (2008). Supply Chain Management: Theory and Practice. Pearson Education.

Davenport, T. H. (2013). Process Innovation: Reengineering Work through Information Technology. Harvard Business Press.

David, F. R. (2017). Strategic Management: Concepts and Cases: Competitiveness and Globalisation (16th ed.). Boston: Pearson.

Drucker, P. F. (1985). Innovation and entrepreneurship: Practice and principles. HarperCollins Publishers.

Eccles, R. G., & Serafeim, G. (2013). The performance frontier: Innovating for a sustainable strategy. Harvard Business Review, 91(5), 50-60.

Edmondson, A. C. (2011). Strategies for Learning from Failure. Harvard Business Review, 89(4), 48-55.

Ford Motor Company. (2006). The Way Forward. https://www.corporate.ford.com/microsites/sustainability-report-2006-07/pdf/2006-7_TheWayForward.pdf

Hitt, M. A., Ireland, R. D., & Hoskisson, R. E. (2016). Strategic management: concepts and cases: competitiveness and globalisation. Cengage Learning.

Hitt, M. A., Ireland, R. D., & Hoskisson, R. E. (2017). Strategic Management: Concepts and Cases: Competitiveness and Globalisation. Boston, MA: Cengage Learning.

Isidore, C. (2009, December 1). Ford's risky bet on small cars is paying off. CNN Business. https://money.cnn.com/2009/12/01/news/companies/ford_small_cars/index.htm

Jacobs, F. R., & Chase, R. B. (2017). Operations and Supply Chain Management. McGraw-Hill Education.

Kaplan, R. S., & Norton, D. P. (2008). The Execution Premium: Linking Strategy to Operations for Competitive Advantage. Boston: Harvard Business Press.

Keller, J., & Richey, K. (2006). The importance of strategic brand management in Starbucks. Journal of Product & Brand Management, 15(7), 473-483.

Kim, W. C., & Mauborgne, R. (2004). Blue ocean strategy. Harvard Business Review, 82(10), 76-84.

Kimmel, P. D., Weygandt, J. J., & Kieso, D. E. (2019). Financial Accounting: Tools for Business Decision Making. Wiley.

Kotler, P., & Keller, K. L. (2016). Marketing Management. Harlow, UK: Pearson Education Limited.

Kotter, J. P. (1990). A Force for Change: How Leadership Differs from Management. Free Press.

Kotter, J. P. (1990). What leaders really do. Harvard Business Review, 68(3), 103-111.

Kotter, J. P. (1996). Leading Change. Harvard Business Press.

Lashinsky, A. (2011). How Starbucks fought for its life without losing its soul. Fortune. https://fortune.com/2011/02/17/how-starbucks-fought-for-its-life-without-losing-its-soul/

Liker, J. K., & Convis, G. L. (2011). The Toyota Way to Continuous Improvement: Linking Strategy and Operational Excellence to Achieve Superior Performance. McGraw-Hill Education.

Locke, E. A., & Latham, G. P. (2002). Building a Practically Useful Theory of Goal Setting and Task Motivation: A 35-Year Odyssey. American Psychologist, 57(9), 705-717.

McKaskill, T. (2019, March 4). Equity Financing: Pros and Cons. Investopedia. https://www.investopedia.com/terms/e/equityfinancing.asp

Mintzberg, H., Ahlstrand, B., & Lampel, J. (2005). Strategy Safari: A Guided Tour Through the Wilds of Strategic Management. New York: Free Press.

Monczka, R. M., Handfield, R. B., Giunipero, L. C., & Patterson, J. L. (2015). Purchasing and Supply Chain Management. Cengage Learning.

Monk, E., & Wagner, B. (2018). Concepts in Enterprise Resource Planning. Cengage Learning.

Osterwalder, A., & Pigneur, Y. (2010). Business Model Generation: A Handbook for Visionaries, Game Changers, and Challengers. John Wiley & Sons.

Osterwalder, A., Pigneur, Y., Bernarda, G., & Smith, A. (2015). Value proposition design: How to create products and services customers want. John Wiley & Sons.

Peng, M. W. (2014). Global strategy (3rd ed.). Cengage Learning.

Porter, M. E. (1980). Competitive Strategy: Techniques for Analysing Industries and Competitors. New York: Free Press.

Porter, M. E. (1985). Competitive Advantage: Creating and Sustaining Superior Performance. New York: Free Press.

Porter, M. E. (1996). What is Strategy? Harvard Business Review, 74(6), 61-78.

Porter, M. E. (1996). What is strategy?. Harvard Business Review, 74(6), 61-78.

Porter, M. E. (1998). Competitive Advantage: Creating and Sustaining Superior Performance. New York: Free Press.

Porter, M. E. (2008). The five competitive forces that shape strategy. Harvard Business Review, 86(1), 25-40.

Ratten, V. (2018). Alternative forms of finance for entrepreneurship and innovation. Journal of Innovation & Knowledge, 3(3), 123-126. https://doi.org/10.1016/j.jik.2018.01.003

Schaper, M., Volery, T., Weber, P. C., & Gibson, B. (2014). Entrepreneurship and Small Business. John Wiley & Sons Australia, Ltd.

Slack, N., Brandon-Jones, A., & Johnston, R. (2019). Operations Management. Pearson.

Spiro, R. L., Stanton, W. J., & Rich, G. A. (2008). Management of a Sales Force. Tata McGraw-Hill Education.

Sutherland, J., & Schwaber, K. (2017). The scrum guide. Scrum.org.

Westerman, G., Bonnet, D., & McAfee, A. (2014). Leading digital: Turning technology into business transformation. Harvard Business Review Press.

Wild, J. J., Shaw, K. W., & Chiappetta, B. (2015). Fundamental Accounting Principles. McGraw-Hill Education.

Womack, J. P., Jones, D. T., & Roos, D. (1990). The Machine That Changed the World. Simon & Schuster